# BOLD,
# BRILLIANT,
# AND
# LATINE

## MEET 52 LATINE AND HISPANIC HEROES FROM PAST AND PRESENT

WIDE EYED EDITIONS

# CONTENTS

# WELCOME, READERS

As an author, Mother, and educator, I know that stories have the power to encourage, educate, and inspire others. This book, *Bold, Brilliant, and Latine*, illuminates and celebrates the lives and legacies of 52 remarkable Latine and Hispanic individuals—some of them you will recognize, and others might be new to you. The goal of this book is for young readers like you to be inspired by the lives and achievements of those who came before you.

You'll meet sports legends, STEM heroes, artists, musicians, activists, political leaders, literary greats, and more. But this is not just a collection of biographies. It's a tribute to the rich tapestry of Latine culture and achievement. As you read, you'll embark on a journey through time and discover individuals who overcame adversity, shattered stereotypes, and defied the odds to make their mark on history. Within, you'll discover stories of resilience, joy, and the power of the human spirit.

As well as plenty of dazzling tales and facts, you'll find a visual feast with colorful and joyful illustrations from ARGENTINIAN artist **Sol Cotti**. Together, Sol and I invite you to celebrate the perseverance, passion, and the extraordinary experiences that have defined the lives of these iconic figures.

That brings me to why I wrote this book. As a writer and a Black Latine queer individual with roots in the Dominican Republic and Puerto Rico, I have dedicated my career to amplifying the voices and narratives society often forgets. It is very important to me to showcase that the Latine community is not one thing. The Latine community is diverse and vibrant, encompassing a wide range of cultures, countries, traditions, dialects, languages, histories, and experiences. By embracing this diversity, we can foster a more inclusive understanding of the Latine identity.

My grandmother was the original storyteller in my life. She only had a second-grade education because she grew up in the Dominican Republic during a time when girls were not educated. Despite this, my abuela was **BOLD** and **BRILLIANT**, and she encouraged me to be bold and brilliant, too. She taught me that every day, I should do three things: one, smile; two, learn something new; and three, help someone in need. I enjoyed writing this book because I could do all of the above every time I sat down to write. I hope it will make you bold and brilliant kiddos smile, learn, and prompt you to discover your own gifts and dreams.

Every child, regardless of their background, should be able to see themselves reflected in the stories they read. Let this book be a reminder that dreams are attainable, no matter who you are or where you come from. Let it be a source of inspiration for the dreamers, the doers, and the young minds eager to shape the world. Let the message that reverberates through each page sink inside you: *"You can be bold, brilliant, and achieve greatness, too."*

Alyssa Reynoso-Morris

Sol Cotti

# VICTORIA MONTOU

**(CIRCA 1739–1805)**

## Freedom Fighter and Healer

**Victoria Montou** was born Abdaraya Toya and is celebrated as a freedom fighter, warrior, midwife, and healer. She is one of the founding mothers of Haiti. Victoria was abducted from her native Dahomey Empire in West Africa (now modern-day Benin) and enslaved and transported to Haiti. Before her enslavement, many believed she was a Dahomey warrior (a member of an all-female elite army known for its courage and combative skills).

In Haiti, Victoria met a young **Jean-Jacques Dessalines**, who later defeated Napoleon's army, proclaimed Haiti's independence, and ruled as its first leader. They were both enslaved on the same plantation. Victoria and Jean were not free to decide how to live their lives. They were forced to work day and night for no money, and they were often beaten and abused. The conditions of slavery were cruel but did not break their spirits.

Victoria trained Jean-Jacques in battle and fought alongside him in the Haitian Revolution. Thanks to Victoria, Jean-Jacques, and countless other freedom fighters like them, Haiti was the first independent country to be established in Latin America and the Caribbean, and the first free Black-led country in the world. The Haitian Revolution was the first successful uprising by enslaved peoples. They created a country free from slavery and ruled by Black and Indigenous former captives.

Jean-Jacques referred to Victoria as his aunty, despite not being related, because she influenced him. Jean-Jacques named her a **Duchess of Haiti** to honor her, and a state funeral fit for a commander was held after her passing.

The all-female army in the popular Black Panther movie was inspired by the Dahomey warriors.

# ANDRÉS BELLO

## Philosopher, diplomat, and poet

CHILE

Say HOLA to **Andrés de Jesús María y José Bello López**—a true polymath, which is a person of wide-ranging knowledge or learning. Born in Venezuela, he became a critical historical figure as a lawmaker, peacekeeper, philosopher, poet, and educator. He studied philosophy, jurisprudence, and medicine at the University of Venezuela in Caracas.

Andrés helped set Venezuela free from the Spanish Empire and then served as a diplomat. The government appointed him to maintain political, economic, and social relations with other countries. He was friends with Simón Bolívar, a Venezuelan military hero who led **South America's independence** from the Spanish Empire. Seeing Andrés' brilliance as a diplomat, the Chilean government asked him to serve as a senator for their country. In that role, he helped write the CHILEAN CIVIL CODE, which are laws governing civil matters, including property rights, family law, and inheritance. The code was so good that many other Latin American countries went on to use it.

Andrés didn't stop there. He served as a professor in Chile and directed several local newspapers. He also helped establish the University of Chile and became its first head for 20 years. His famous poetry collection, *Silvas Americanas,* was made up of two epic poems that describe the awe-inspiring South American landscape. His writing explored subjects like law and philosophy. An avid philologist (student of languages), he studied the history of languages and published a book about grammar. Andrés was a true master of many skills—**a real-life superhero**!

# FRANCISCO MORAZÁN

**José Francisco Morazán Quesada** was a liberal politician from Central America. He was born in present-day Honduras during a time when Spanish colonial rule was dwindling. Growing up, Francisco was a big reader. He learned about the French Revolution and other moments of social change in history, which inspired him.

He joined the military as a young man and fought on the side of the liberals, who wanted a united and secular Central America. He led troops at the **Battle of La Trinidad** and captured Honduras from his enemies. Three years later, he was elected as President of the Federal Republic of Central America. This consisted of the present-day southern Mexican state of Chiapas along with Costa Rica, El Salvador, Guatemala, Honduras, Nicaragua, and Belize.

Francisco was hailed as a visionary and brilliant thinker in his efforts to unite Central America into a single, developed nation. He established liberal reforms, including freedom of the press, expression, and religion. Under his leadership, the republic built schools and roads, and welcomed immigrants.

Francisco also limited the power of the Catholic church by making marriage secular, authorizing divorce, and legalizing homosexuality. His politics angered powerful enemies. They wanted to divide Central America into five separate nations that they could govern with their own (more conservative) beliefs, and eventually, they succeeded. Francisco was captured and sentenced to death. Despite his tragic end, he died a hero to many, and his legacy of unity within Latin America is a goal many modern leaders continue to strive toward.

FEDERAL REPUBLIC OF CENTRAL AMERICA

REPÚBLICA FEDERAL DE CENTRO AMÉRICA

*Central American Politician and Unifier*

# GABRIELA MISTRAL

**(1889–1957)**

**Gabriela Mistral** was also known as Lucila Godoy Alcayaga. Gabriela not only had two names, but she also wore many hats during a time when most women were not in positions of power or influence: She was a poet, educator, and diplomat. Gabriela and her family struggled with poverty after her father left them when she was only three years old. As an adult, she started working as a teacher to help support her mother.

As well as teaching, Gabriela wrote poetry using a pen name. She became the first Latin American to win a NOBEL PRIZE in Literature. Gabriela's writing explores love, sorrow, nature, travel, and love for children. Her most famous works include *Desolación (Desolation)* in 1922 and *Ternura (Tenderness)* in 1924. She often celebrated the strength and gentleness of women in her work. She is especially known for her use of free verse, which is when poems do not follow traditional poetic rules and elements. In free verse, poets have the freedom to write in a way that allows for more flexibility and expression.

Gabriela said, *"I write poetry because I can't disobey the impulse; it would be like blocking a spring that surges up in my throat."*

Gabriela was also a Chilean diplomat and held positions in various countries. She worked hard for causes close to her heart and she advocated for access to literacy and education for children, especially in rural areas. She taught Spanish literature at Columbia University, Vassar College, Middlebury College, the University of Puerto Rico, and many more international institutions.

Today, Gabriela is fondly remembered for her verses, feminist ideologies, and passion for education.

CHILE

*The Poet, Teacher, and Diplomat*

# MATILDE HIDALGO

**(1889–1974)**

ECUADOR

## La Primera—Trailblazing Doctor, Feminist, and Politician

**Matilde Hidalgo Navarro de Procel** was a trailblazer! She was Ecuador's first female high-school graduate, the country's inaugural female doctor, the first woman to cast a vote in Latin America, and the first woman to be elected to public office. Before changing the course of history, however, she faced adversity.

Matilde loved school but was denied an education after sixth grade simply because she was a girl. Undeterred, she fought for the right to attend the local boys' high school, even though the community disapproved. Mothers prevented their daughters from being her friend and the local priest didn't allow her inside the church. Still, her persistence paid off, and she became the first girl in Ecuador to graduate from high school. This was just the beginning! Time and again Matilde faced injustice simply for being a woman, but she never backed down. She pursued a medical degree and went on

to become Ecuador's first female doctor. As a practicing doctor, Matilde used her education to find a loophole in the Constitution of Ecuador and become the first woman to vote there—and in all of Latin America! When her application to vote was questioned, she argued that the Constitution only required voters to be 21-year-old Ecuadorian citizens who could read and write—which she was. The State Council unanimously accepted her argument, marking a historic moment.

Matilde went on to become the first female candidate and the first elected Council Member in Ecuador; she later served as Vice President of the Council. Her legacy is celebrated at the **Museo de Matilde Hidalgo de Procel** in Loja, showcasing her achievements in medicine and the women's suffrage movement. Matilde is an inspiration for future generations to never give up!

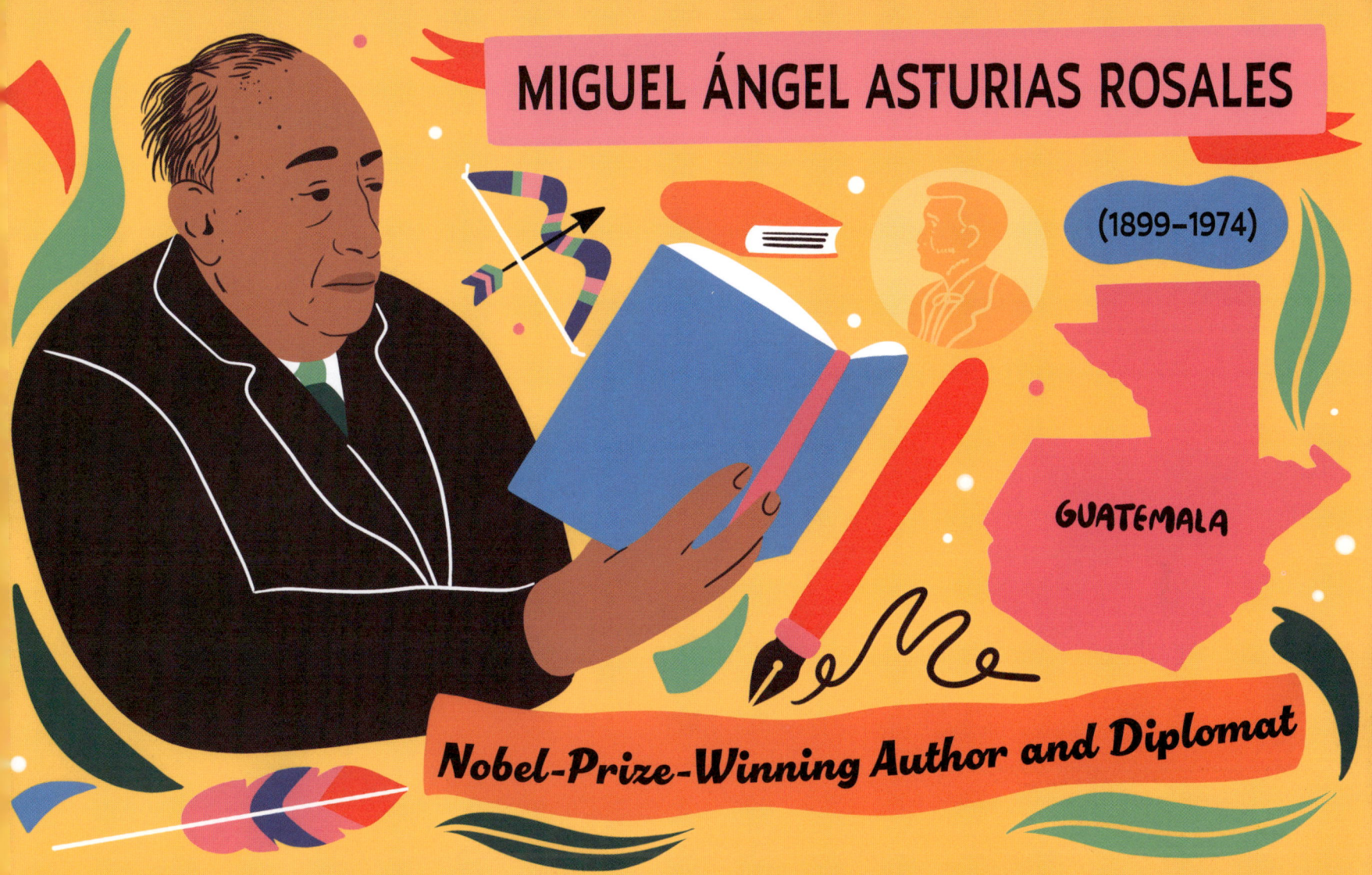

# MIGUEL ÁNGEL ASTURIAS ROSALES

**(1899–1974)**

GUATEMALA

## Nobel-Prize-Winning Author and Diplomat

**Miguel Ángel Asturias Rosales** was a remarkable Guatemalan diplomat, poet, novelist, playwright, and journalist who used his writing to illuminate the stories of indigenous cultures.

When Miguel Ángel was six years old, his father lost his job due to a clash with a dictator called Manuel Estrada Cabrera. His family moved to his grandparents' farm, where Miguel Ángel met his nanny, Lola Reyes. Lola was a young Indigenous woman, and she shared wonderful myths and legends from her culture with Miguel Ángel, inspiring much of his later writing.

Miguel Ángel attended high school and law school at the University of San Carlos. He was among a group of students who founded the Popular University of Guatemala, offering courses to people who couldn't afford a traditional university education. Always wanting to learn more, Miguel Ángel ventured to Europe to continue his studies and, while in Paris, was inspired by lectures about Mayan religions.

Miguel Ángel always stood up for the causes he believed in, becoming a prominent voice against dictatorship and the exploitation of indigenous people. His activism meant he spent much of his later life in exile from his home country. Miguel Ángel's novel *El Señor Presidente (Mr President)*, which describes life under a dictator, took over thirteen years to publish because of dictator Jorge Ubico. *Hombres de maíz (Men of Maize)* explores the devastating effects of big businesses and capitalism on Guatemalan people, customs, and ancestral beliefs.

After years fighting for justice, Miguel Ángel's efforts were recognized. He became the second Latin American author to receive the NOBEL PRIZE in Literature and won the Soviet Union's Lenin Peace Prize.

Miguel Ángel Asturias Rosales used his words not only to protect people's rights but also to honor their culture.

# MANUEL ÁLVAREZ BRAVO

**(1902–2002)**

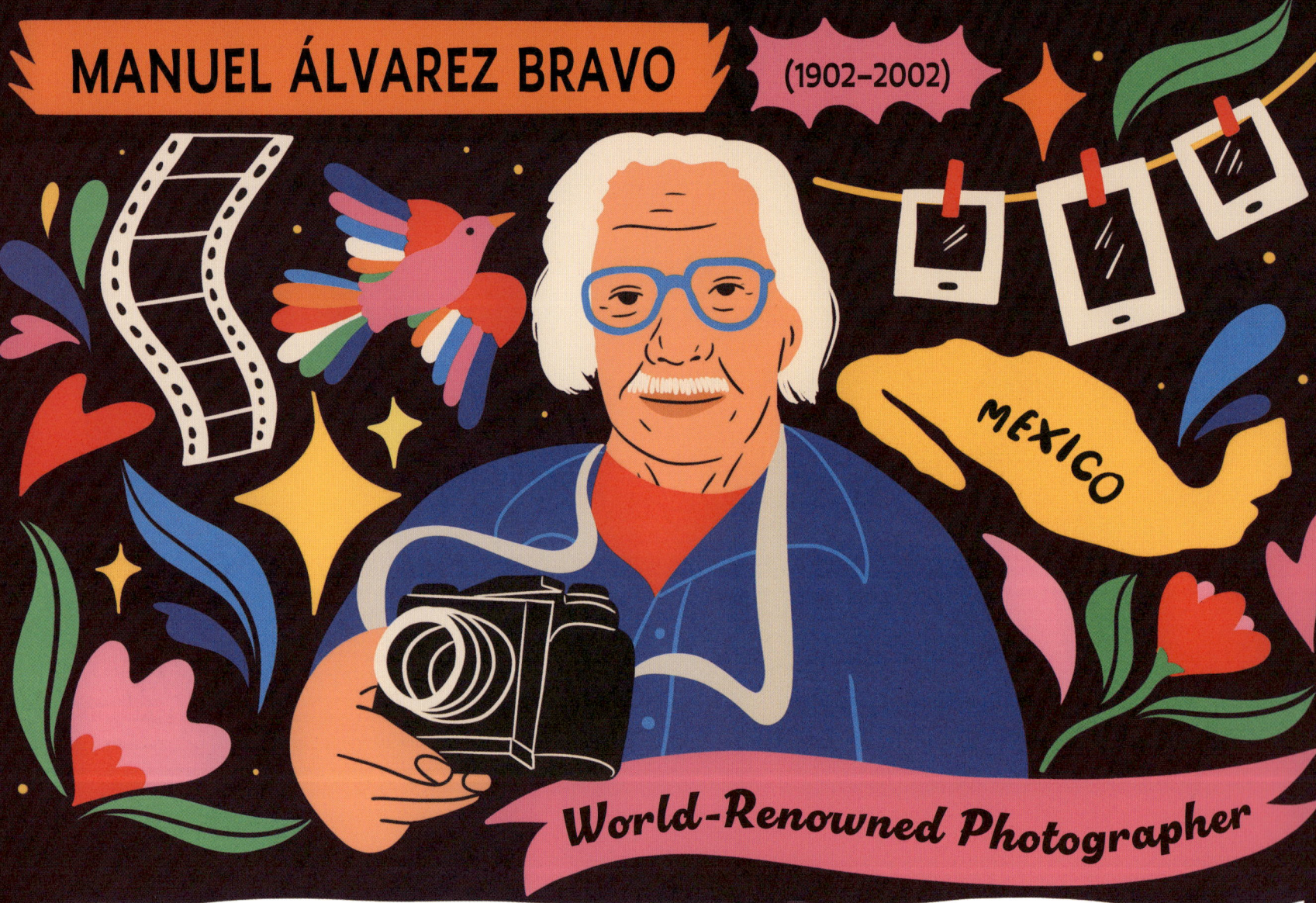

MEXICO

## World-Renowned Photographer

**Manuel Álvarez Bravo** was a photographer born and raised in Mexico City, where creativity swirled all around him. His father was a teacher who loved painting, making music, and plays. Even his grandpa made portraits. But life wasn't easy. Manuel grew up as the Mexican Revolution was unfolding. He heard gunfire and witnessed violence, which would later influence his work. Then, when he was 12, tragedy struck: His dad passed away and he had to leave school.

Manuel worked in a textile factory and studied accounting, but he switched to painting classes because his heart belonged to the arts.

He taught himself photography and was offered advice from great photographers of the time. Manuel's photographs captured the ordinary, and his subjects were related to everyday life, folk art, and rituals. He had a special talent for capturing Mexican culture, regular working people, and Indigenous peoples. His work was showcased in exhibitions worldwide and featured in many publications.

Manuel founded **the Fondo Editorial de la Plástica Mexicana** to produce books on Mexican art, highlighting the talent of other artists. He won dozens of awards, including a Guggenheim Fellowship, the Master of Photography Prize from the International Center of Photography, and recognition by **UNESCO**. He also worked in Mexican cinema and taught the next generation of photographers.

We should all hope to be more like Manuel. He is a lesson to follow our dreams, seek out supportive mentors, and give back to future generations.

# FRIDA KAHLO

**(1907–1954)**

MEXICO

Magdalena Carmen Frida Kahlo y Calderón, known as **Frida Kahlo**, was an extraordinary Mexican painter who created beautiful and thought-provoking artwork. She is famous for her self-portraits that reflect her Mexican heritage and personal experiences. Her unique style blended reality with imagination. She used vibrant colors and was influenced by nature, Mexican artifacts, and folk art. Through her art, she explored important topics like identity, gender, class, and race.

As a child, Frida was affected by polio, which inspired her to pursue medical school. But her life plans changed drastically when she was 18. She was in a terrible bus accident that caused her lifelong pain and medical problems. However, her recovery led her back to her childhood love of art.

Frida was not only an artist but a political activist. She joined the Mexican Communist Party, working to prioritize the interests of the working class. She met other artists and friends who shared her interests and politics, including her husband and fellow-artist Diego Rivera.

Frida's unique portraits caught the attention of art enthusiasts worldwide, and were displayed in the famous Louvre Museum in Paris.

Despite her health struggles, Frida continued to paint and teach art. She became an icon for many groups, including Chicanos, feminists, Indigenous peoples, and the LGBTQ＊ community.

Frida's paintings are like windows into her soul, showing her passion for her roots and determination to overcome challenges. She remains a true inspiration for artists and dreamers of all ages!

*Iconic and Rebellious Painter*

# ALEJANDRO ZAFFARONI

(1923–2014)

## Super Inventor, Biochemist, Entrepreneur, and Mentor

URUGUAY

**Alejandro Zaffaroni** was a Uruguayan super inventor, which means he made A LOT of new appliances, machines, and processes. In fact, he was granted over 45 patents and was inducted into the National Inventors Hall of Fame.

Alejandro was a successful entrepreneur. He founded several companies in Silicon Valley in California. Many entrepreneurs and scientists called him a kind, encouraging mentor, pouring his energy and expertise into the next generation.

Alejandro also studied biochemistry, which is a type of science that combines natural sciences and chemistry. He received a scholarship through the Institute of International Education to study in the United States. After he graduated, he started many companies, including DNAX, Affymax, Symyx Technologies, Maxygen, SurroMed, and Affymetrix. The products he developed were birth control pills, the nicotine patch, corticosteroids, and more. He developed DNA chips, which allowed many genes to be examined simultaneously. They are now used to find genetic variants linked to different diseases.

Alejandro's legacy is one of investing in the next generation. He helped dozens of scientists and entrepreneurs. He and his wife, Lida, donated to various scientific causes, including a breast imaging center at Stanford University. A $10 million financial aid program for Latin American students was established at Stanford in his honor. To recognize and honor his incredible contribution to the world of STEM, in 1995, Alejandro was awarded **the U.S. National Medal of Technology and Innovation**.

# MIRABAL SISTERS

## (1924–1960)

Patria

Minerva

María Teresa

Some hero stories are sad, and this is one of them. But it is essential to tell the stories of the **Mirabal sisters** (codename "Las Mariposas," or "Butterflies") because their sacrifices liberated the Dominican Republic (DR) and inspired women all over the world to stand up against violence.

There were four Mirabal sisters, three of whom (Patria, Minerva, and María Teresa) opposed the brutal 31-year dictatorship of US ally Rafael Trujillo (nicknamed El Jefe). The three sisters were violently assassinated on November 25, 1960. The last sister, Adela (or Dedé), who wasn't politically involved, passed away of natural causes many years later.

Minerva was the most politically active, as she founded the June 14 Revolutionary Movement with her husband, Manolo Tavárez Justo. María Teresa was the youngest sister to become involved. The older sister, Patria, was less active but supported her sisters. She let the revolutionaries use her house to store weapons and tools.

Trujillo ruled the DR with violence. His forces murdered his critics, and he banned other political parties. After 30 years of oppression, Trujillo's regime was being challenged, and he publicly stated that he had only two problems: the Catholic Church and the Mirabal sisters. Trujillo hated the sisters because they threatened him

politically and personally. He was furious at Minerva for rejecting him romantically. Enraged by their criticism, he wanted to silence them. Trujillo's agents murdered the sisters and threw their car off a cliff to simulate an accident. The murder sparked outrage and fueled opposition to Trujillo, and he was assassinated six months later.

The tireless work of their surviving sister, Dedé, made the women national icons. Their legacy was honored in 1999 when November 25 was designated as **the International Day for the Elimination of Violence against Women** by the United Nations. May we honor and protect women everywhere, every day.

# CELIA CRUZ

(1925–2003)

CUBA

The Queen of Salsa!

16

**Celia Cruz** was born Úrsula Hilaria Celia de la Caridad Cruz Alfonso in Havana, Cuba, and her life was as festive as her music. Her father was a railway stoker and her mother was a housewife. Celia was among the oldest of 14 children living in the house, including cousins and siblings.

According to her mother, she began singing as a child before her first birthday, and in time she went on to be an international sensation. She was part of a famous Cuban music group called Sonora Matancera for 15 years. She could sing various music styles, from guaracha to rumba, afro, son, and bolero.

Then, the Cuban Revolution changed everything. She had publicly spoken against President Fidel Castro and worried she would be arrested. Some people believe that Fidel was a good leader because he made sure everyone had access to education and healthcare. But others, like Celia, felt he didn't let people speak freely or have different ideas. She left Cuba in 1960, not knowing if she would ever come back. When she tried to return to visit her sick mother, she was denied entry.

She continued her music journey in Mexico and then in the United States. She sang with other famous artists and recorded lively and joyful hit songs like "**La vida es un carnaval.**" Celia makes every Latino proud, especially Black Latinos, for representing her African ancestry with pride in songs like "**Azucar Negra.**" She also tackled issues like machismo culture (the idea that men are better than women and that boys should always be tough, strong, and not show their feelings) through her songs.

She was a music legend, with 37 studio albums, over 10 million records sold, and many awards, including multiple Grammys and the National Endowment for the Arts award. In fact, she didn't just sing—she acted in movies and telenovelas too! Celia's catchphrase "**¡Azúcar!**", which means sugar, became a symbol of salsa music. It was her unique way of spreading joy, sweetness, and energy to her audience.

Celia Cruz's music is like a fiesta that never ends. She brought joy to people all around the world. So, if you ever want to dance and feel the rhythm, just put on some Celia Cruz and let the "*Queen of Salsa*" take you away!

# GABRIEL GARCÍA MÁRQUEZ

**(1927–2014)**

## Nobel-Prize-Winning Author and Father of Magical Realism

**Gabriel José de la Concordia García Márquez** was a journalist and author born in the small town of Aracataca, Colombia. His father became a pharmacist and moved with his mom, leaving Gabriel to be raised by his grandparents for the first years of his life.

Gabriel became famous for using a style of writing and books called **MAGICAL REALISM**, in which fantastical things happen in regular, everyday places. One of his favorite made-up towns was **MACONDO**, which is similar to his hometown of Aracataca. His stories have been translated into many different languages.

As a journalist, he never hesitated in his criticism of Colombian and foreign politics. He was liberal in his views like his grandfather. In fact, his grandparents influenced his popular novel *One Hundred Years of Solitude*. His grandfather, a liberal veteran of the Thousand Days' War, was well-known for refusing to remain silent about the Banana Massacre (when the Colombian government killed thousands of United Fruit Company workers who were striking for better conditions). Gabriel was also inspired by how his grandmother *"treated the extraordinary as something perfectly natural."* The house was filled with stories of ghosts and premonitions. He enjoyed his grandmother's fantastical way of telling stories, which is the core of magical realism.

In 1982, Gabriel was the first Colombian (and fourth Latin American) to win a **NOBEL PRIZE** for Literature for *"his novels and short stories, in which the fantastic and the realistic are combined in a richly composed world of imagination, reflecting a continent's life and conflicts."*

COLOMBIA

Cesar Estrada Chavez was an American labor leader and civil rights hero who stood tall for farm workers. Born in Arizona to a Mexican-American family, Cesar started life as a farm boy. Little did he know he would grow up to become a legend!

When Cesar was 11, his family lost their farm during the Great Depression. They were forced to become migrant farm workers (farmers that travel and work on other farms). They were exploited and treated unjustly. They worked long hours, were underpaid, and didn't have rights to protect them.

Motivated by his experiences, Cesar decided he wanted to be a part of a movement for change. He joined **the Community Service Organization**

**(CSO)**, whom he worked with for 10 years. There, he coordinated voter registration drives to get people to vote, led campaigns against racial and economic discrimination, and organized new CSO chapters across California.

Cesar's dream was to organize a union to protect and serve farm workers. He met social justice warrior Dolores Huerta at a CSO event and they teamed up. Dolores co-founded a CSO charter and founded the Agricultural Workers Association because, as a teacher, she saw too many farm children coming to school hungry. She wanted to help them by organizing farmers and farm workers.

Together, Cesar and Dolores established **the National Farm**

**Workers Association**, which became **the United Farm Workers' Union (UFW)**. This heroic duo fought for justice and fairness for farm workers. For years, they organized peaceful protests, hunger strikes, and boycotts to demand better pay, safer working conditions, and respect for farm workers. Their hard work didn't go unnoticed. Cesar and Dolores were honored with many awards, including the Presidential Medal of Freedom.

Even though Cesar passed away in 1993, his legacy lives on. His birthday, March 31, is celebrated as **Cesar Chavez Day**, reminding us to stand up for what's right. Remember, no matter how small you are, you can make a BIG difference in the world, just like Cesar and his great friend Dolores!

(1927–1993)

# CESAR CHAVEZ

U.S.A.

## The Hero of Farm Workers

Meet **Rita Moreno**, an award-winning actress, dancer, and singer for over 70 years. She was the third person in history and the first Latina to achieve the coveted EGOT status, earning all four major entertainment awards: Emmy, Grammy, Oscar, and Tony. She also boasts the Triple Crown of Acting, which includes the Academy, Emmy, and Tony awards.

Rita was born Rosa Dolores Alverío Marcano in Humacao, Puerto Rico. Her mother was a seamstress and her father was a farmer. When she was only five years old, she and her mother moved to New York City. In the bustling city, Rita took dance classes that would shape her future.

When she was only 11, she was hired to record Spanish-language versions of American films. Soon after, she debuted on Broadway aged 13, playing Angelina in *Skydrift*. Next, she played supporting roles in musicals *Singin' in the Rain* and *The King and I*. However, her breakout role came when she portrayed Anita in *West Side Story* in 1961, earning her the Best Supporting Actress Academy Award the following year.

Rita's cinematic journey continued with roles in notable films such as *The Four Seasons*, and *I Like It Like That*. On stage, she wowed audiences as Googie Gomez in *The Ritz*, winning the Tony Award for Best Featured Actress in a Musical. Rita earned a Grammy for *The Electric Company Album*. She also won two consecutive Emmy Awards for her roles on *The Muppet Show* and *The Rockford Files*.

In 2021, her incredible life story was celebrated in the documentary *Rita Moreno: Just a Girl Who Decided to Go for It*. Her achievements include the Presidential Medal of Freedom, the National Medal of Arts, and the Screen Actors Guild Life Achievement Award. Rita's extraordinary journey inspires us all, proving that we can achieve greatness with talent, determination, and a fearless spirit. May we all aspire to do what we love, like Rita!

RITA MORENO

(1931–PRESENT)

PUERTO RICO

Award-Winning Actress, Dancer, and Singer

# OSCAR DE LA RENTA

## (1932–2014)

DOMINICAN REPUBLIC

### World-Renowned Fashion Designer and Humanitarian

**Oscar de la Renta** was born Óscar Arístides Renta Fiallo in Santo Domingo, Dominican Republic (DR), and took the fashion world by storm. He designed high-class couture collections for world-renowned fashion houses. He dressed American First Ladies and celebrities like Oprah. His legacy lives on through his signature **ready-to-wear** collections, including women's evening wear, suits, and bridal gowns.

At the age of 18, Oscar studied painting in Spain at **the Royal Academy of San Fernando** in Madrid. For extra money, he drew clothes for newspapers and fashion houses. A dress he sketched appeared on the cover of *Life* magazine, which helped him land apprenticeships with renowned couturiers like Spain's Cristóbal Balenciaga and Antonio del Castillo at Lanvin in Paris. He then worked for Arden in New York and designed the couture collection for the house of Balmain.

An avid gardener, Oscar's dresses and suits often boasted brightly colored flower prints and embroidery. His style was simple with a modern pop. He often used lace, ruffles, bows, beads, sequins, and metallic threads as embellishments.

Oscar was also a humanitarian, always giving his passion to causes that spoke to him. In DR, he founded the Casa del Niño orphanage, funded the construction of schools, and was the Ambassador-at-Large. He was a board member of the Metropolitan Opera, Carnegie Hall, and New Yorkers for Children. He participated in Designed for a Cure 2014 to raise money for the Cancer Center at the University of Miami.

His extensive list of accomplishments includes induction into the Coty Hall of Fame and the International Best Dressed List Hall of Fame. He received the Council of Fashion Designers of America, Inc. Lifetime Achievement Award, and the Carnegie Hall Medal of Excellence.

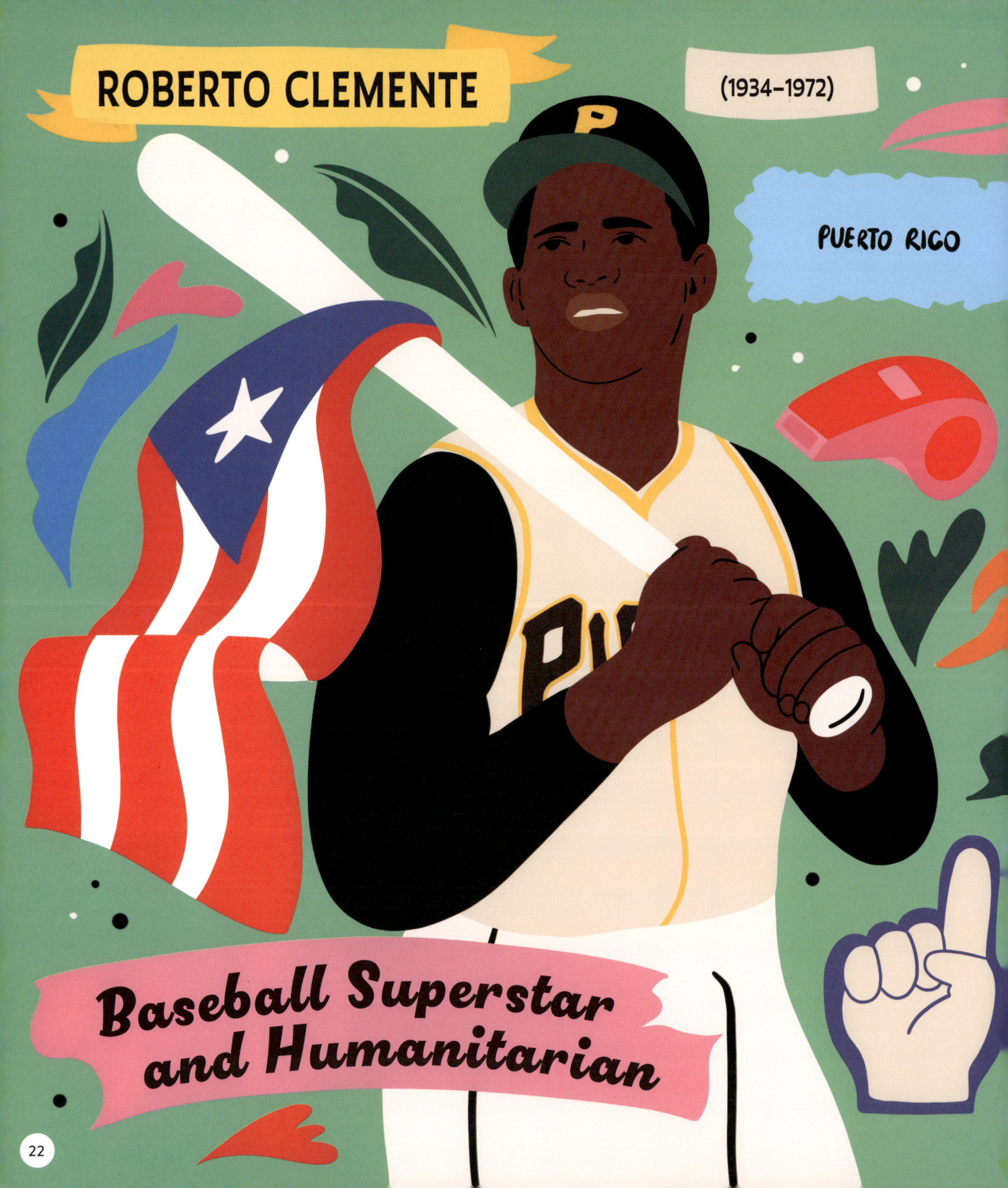

ROBERTO CLEMENTE (1934–1972)

PUERTO RICO

Baseball Superstar and Humanitarian

**Roberto Enrique Clemente Walker** was a legendary Puerto Rican baseball player. He made his mark on the sport during an incredible 18-SEASON career in Major League Baseball.

Roberto was the youngest of seven siblings. He worked with his father in the sugar cane fields. They had little money, but this didn't stop Roberto from dreaming big. He aspired to be an Olympic track and field star, but committed to baseball when he was 14 years old.

Roberto joined Puerto Rico's amateur league with the Ferdinand Juncos team. At age 18, he accepted a contract with the **Puerto Rican Professional Baseball League**. His career began to soar, and he was recruited by the Brooklyn Dodgers before finding his home with the Pittsburgh Pirates. As a Black Latino, Roberto faced discrimination throughout his baseball career, but he always remained true to his heritage, overcoming prejudice and fighting stereotypes.

Roberto's sporting accomplishments were remarkable—he was a 13-TIME All-Star, a **Gold Glove Award** winner for 12 SEASONS in a row, and a TWO-TIME **World Series champion**. Breaking barriers, he became the first Caribbean and Latin American player to win a World Series as a starting position player, as well as the first to receive a National League *and* a World Series Most Valuable Player Award. Off the field, Roberto was a beacon of generosity, delivering food and baseball equipment to those in need in Latin America and the Caribbean.

Tragically, Roberto lost his life when he was just 38 years old. He died in a plane crash while on his way to Nicaragua to deliver aid after an earthquake. In honor of his legacy, the Pirates retired his uniform (number 21). The National Baseball Hall of Fame changed its eligibility rules, and he became the first Caribbean and Latin American player to be celebrated there.

Roberto Clemente's extraordinary achievements inspire future generations to embody the spirit of sport and give back to their communities whenever possible.

# MARIO VARGAS LLOSA

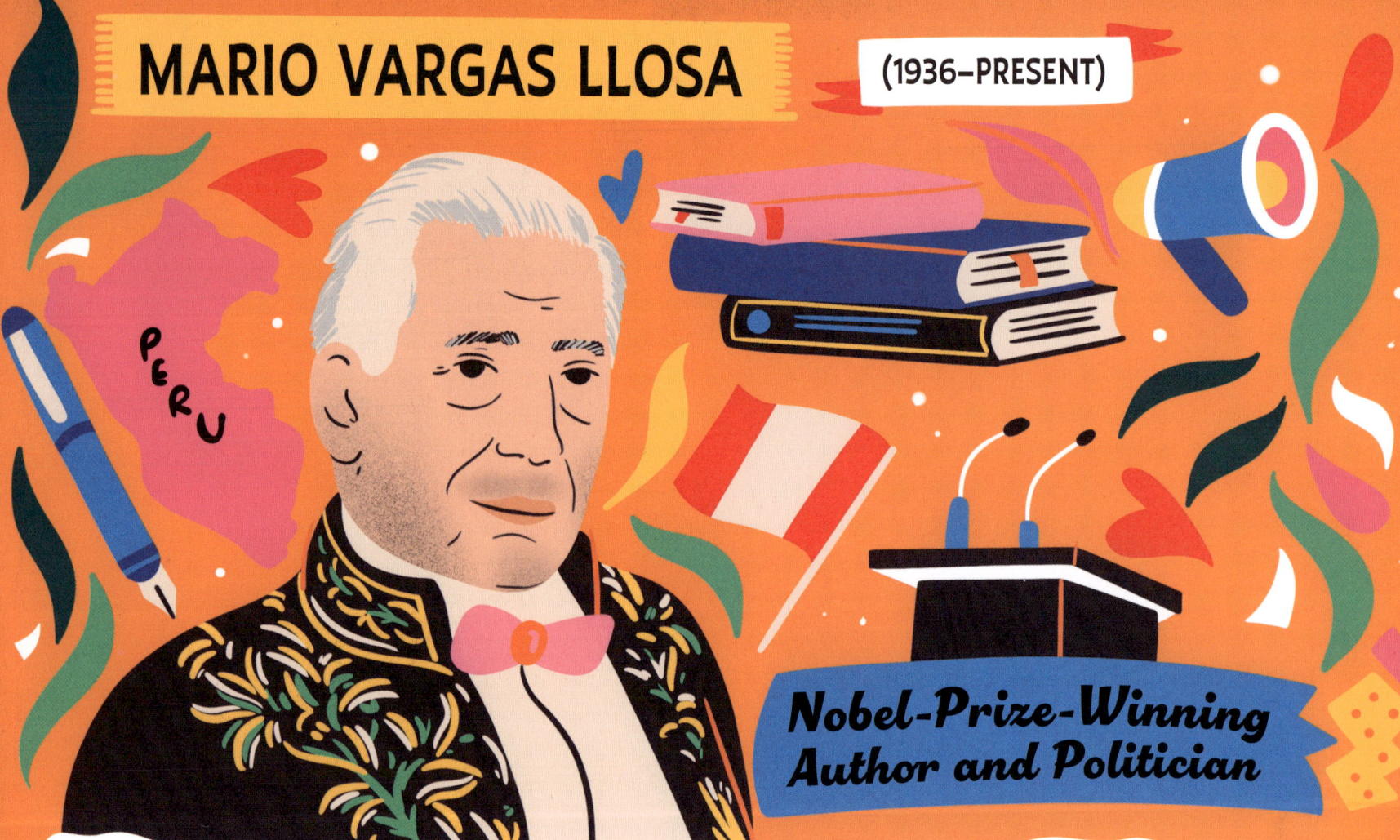

PERU

**Nobel-Prize-Winning Author and Politician**

**Mario Vargas Llosa** is a Peruvian author, journalist, and politician. Born Jorge Mario Pedro Vargas Llosa, he grew up in Peru and Bolivia with his mother and maternal grandparents. His parents separated before he was born, and Mario always believed that his father had passed away until a surprise meeting when he was ten years old reunited the two of them.

Mario's writing career began at just 16 years old, when he worked as an amateur journalist for local newspapers. He went on to study law and literature at the National University of San Marcos. He soon published his first short stories and saw his very first play, *La huida del Inca*, performed on stage.

He became a prolific author, writing comedies, murder mysteries, historical novels, and political thrillers. *The Time of the Hero* is a famous novel about adolescents in a Peruvian military school, striving to survive in a hostile and violent environment.

*The Green House*, set in the Peruvian jungle, uses dream-like elements to capture its characters' broken realities. Several of his works have even been turned into movies.

Beyond his success as an author, Mario was also a politically active young man. He joined a communist group at university and initially supported the Cuban revolutionary government of Fidel Castro, inspired by the leader's fight against corruption and inequality. He later changed his mind and disagreed with Castro's policies to silence opposition and limit freedom of speech. Mario even ran for the Peruvian presidency.

Mario's impact on culture and community has been celebrated with a huge number of awards, including the **NOBEL PRIZE** in Literature, and the **Pablo Neruda Order of Artistic and Cultural Merit**. He continues to inspire minds through his captivating stories and his commitment to equality.

# CAROLINA HERRERA

**(1939–PRESENT)**

## Fashion Designer Extraordinaire

**Carolina Herrera** is a famous fashion designer from Venezuela. Her clothing has been loved by all kinds of celebrities, as well as First Ladies Michelle Obama and Jackie Onassis Kennedy. Her designs stand out from the crowd for their grace, elegance, and femininity. She lives by the motto *"alegría de vivir,"* which means *"the joy of living."*

Carolina's father was an Air Force Officer and the Governor of Caracas, the capital city of Venezuela, but it was her grandmother who first introduced her to the world of fashion. She took Carolina to shows by Balenciaga, the famous Spanish fashion house, and bought her outfits from French fashion houses like Lanvin and Dior. Carolina said, *"My eye was accustomed to seeing pretty things."*

Before becoming a designer herself, Carolina developed a reputation for her dramatic style,

including her love of bold shapes and simple colors. In 1972, she appeared on the International Best-Dressed List, and in 1980, she was elected to its Hall of Fame. Soon afterwards, her friend Diana Vreeland, Editor-in-Chief of *Vogue*, suggested that she design her own clothing line. Carolina did just that, and she received recognition from several famous publications, including **Women's Wear Daily** and **Tatler**.

This fashion superstar has been on the cover of *Vogue* an amazing SEVEN times, and she has earned an array of awards, including the Geoffrey Beene Lifetime Achievement Award from the Council of Fashion Designers of America, and the Fashion Group International Superstar Award. Carolina's stand-out sense of style continues to be an inspiration to fashionistas everywhere.

# ÓSCAR ARIAS SÁNCHEZ

(1940–PRESENT)

**Óscar Arias Sánchez** served as president of Costa Rica not once but twice! He was awarded the Nobel Peace Prize for his efforts to stop conflicts across Central America.

Óscar excelled in school and he went on to enroll at Boston University to study medicine. However, he soon decided to head home and instead completed degrees in law and economics at the University of Costa Rica. He loved to learn, and continued to study at various other institutions. He has also received over FIFTY honorary doctorates from renowned universities including Harvard and Princeton.

He successfully ran for president in 1986 and used his knowledge of economics to diversify Costa Rica's economy, which meant that the country could make money from a wider range of activities. He often met with citizens one-to-one and made sure to listen to their concerns.

Óscar's most outstanding achievement was his plan to bring peace and political stability to Central America during a time of turmoil and violence. In the late 1970s, civil wars and revolutions were devastating many countries in the region, including El Salvador and Guatemala. The area was also caught up in the Cold War, which led to interference in the region's affairs. Óscar's plan protected democracy and human rights by calling for a stop to fighting between governments and rebel forces, as well as ending foreign interference. It was supported by Costa Rica, Guatemala, El Salvador, Honduras, and Nicaragua.

The plan was recognized with the **Nobel Peace Prize** in 1987, and Óscar also received the **Albert Schweitzer Prize** for Humanitarianism. His presidencies are remembered for championing equality and fighting corruption.

COSTA RICA

## Two-Time President and Promoter of Peace

# ISABEL ALLENDE

Renowned Chilean-American author **Isabel Allende** has captivated millions of readers around the world with her imaginative storytelling. In 1943, Isabel was born Isabel Angelica Allende Llona in Lima, Peru. She grew up in Chile and moved to the U.S. in the 1980s.

Her family was exiled from Chile after her uncle, Chilean President Salvador Allende, was overthrown in a military coup. Their experience fleeing to Venezuela inspired Isabel to write her first novel, *The House of the Spirits*. Published in 1982, it became an instant bestseller and catapulted her to international fame.

Since then, Isabel has sold over 77 million copies of her 26 bestselling and critically acclaimed books. Her writing is known for its rich imagery, magical realism, and passionate characters who grapple with complex social issues and personal struggles.

Isabel is also a passionate activist and humanitarian. Following the death of her daughter Paula, in 1996 she founded **the Isabel Allende Foundation**, which protects women and girls, and empowers them to achieve economic independence, reproductive rights, and freedom from violence. She also holds 15 international honorary doctorates, including one from Harvard University, showing how respected she is worldwide.

Isabel's literature and social justice contributions have earned her more than 60 awards from over 15 countries, including the PRESIDENTIAL MEDAL OF FREEDOM from President Barack Obama, the **National Book Award**, and **Chile's National Literature Prize**. She continues to inspire readers and advocates worldwide with her powerful storytelling and unwavering commitment to social justice.

CHILE

" When I was young, I often felt desperate: so much pain in the world and so little I could do to alleviate it! But now I look back at my life and feel satisfied, because few days went by without me at least trying to make a difference. "

Author and Activist

# MARIO MOLINA

## (1943–2020)

MEXICO

**Mario José Molina-Pasquel Henríquez** was the first Mexican-born scientist to receive a **NOBEL PRIZE** in Chemistry. He contributed to one of the most important discoveries ever made in environmental science.

Mario was born in Mexico City and he had a passion for math and science from a very young age. While his parents weren't scientists themselves, they both encouraged his interests, even allowing Mario to convert the family bathroom into a science lab! Fortunately, his aunt was an established chemist and she helped him with all kinds of challenging scientific experiments.

He went to boarding school in Switzerland when he was 11 and later enrolled in the chemical engineering program at the National Autonomous University of Mexico. He continued to study and was rewarded with positions at the University of California, the California Institute of Technology, the Massachusetts Institute of Technology, and the Center for Atmospheric Sciences.

His stand-out discovery revealed the workings of the **ozone** (a layer in the Earth's atmosphere that protects our planet from the Sun's UV rays). Mario found that certain gases, such as chlorofluorocarbons (CFCs), can break down and deplete the ozone, putting our planet at risk. This theory of ozone depletion changed people's attitude towards CFCs and showed that humans need to limit how much we use them.

Mario was the director of the **Mario Molina Center for Energy and Environment** in Mexico City. He served as a climate policy advisor to the President of Mexico, Enrique Peña Nieto, and was also an advisor to President Barack Obama.

Mario's love of chemistry started at a young age and he stuck with it, showing us that we should always follow our passions!

## Nobel-Prize-Winning Chemist and Climate Change Advisor

Antonia Coello Novello is a trailblazer in medicine and public health. Born in Puerto Rico, she faced many challenges when she was young, including the loss of her father.

She also had a health condition called "congenital megacolon," which left her feeling tired and unable to do certain activities. Her mother worked as a school teacher and principal, and didn't have a lot of money. They couldn't afford the surgery Antonia needed to cure her condition until she was 18 years old. But she never gave up!

These experiences, along with her mother emphasizing the importance of education and caring for others, motivated Antonia to become a doctor. She wanted to help sick children struggling to access healthcare.

She felt compelled to make a difference on a large scale, and that's just what she did. Throughout her career, she made widespread improvements to healthcare, working in **AIDS and HIV prevention** and helping to change laws around organ transplants. She also contributed to rules about health warnings on cigarette packaging, making a big difference to the health of whole communities.

Antonia's good work caught the attention of President George H.W. Bush, who appointed her as the first woman (and the first Latina) Surgeon General of the United States in 1990, a senior role protecting and promoting healthcare.

Even after she retired, Antonia provided medical care in Puerto Rico following Hurricane Maria, and advocated for COVID-19 vaccine access for communities of color. She earned numerous awards, including the **Public Health Service Commendation Medal** and the **Congressional Hispanic Caucus Medal**.

Antonia used her skills to make the world a healthier place for everyone. Her inspiring journey teaches us about the importance of perseverance, education, and commitment.

# ANTONIA NOVELLO

(1944–PRESENT)

PUERTO RICO

## First Woman and First Latina to Become Surgeon General of the United States

# JUAN GABRIEL

## Singer, Songwriter, and Superstar

MEXICO

**Juan Gabriel** was an extraordinarily talented Mexican singer, songwriter, and actor with over **40 MILLION** records sold worldwide. Born Alberto Aguilera Valadez, Juan Gabriel did not have an easy start in life. His father was hospitalized when he was two and, since his mother couldn't afford to look after him, he was raised in an orphanage. It was here that he developed an interest in music, composing his first song at just 13!

Juan Gabriel faced many hurdles on his journey to stardom, including rejections from record companies, and times when he had to sleep in bus and train stations. He was even wrongfully accused of stealing, which led to a year and a half in prison. During this time, his songs caught the attention of the prison warden, who introduced him to Mexican singer and actor La Prieta Linda. With her support, he signed a record deal using the stage name Juan Gabriel to honor his father, Gabriel, and teacher, Juan.

Juan Gabriel wrote around 1,800 songs across many different genres, from ranchera and ballads to pop, rock, and disco. His first album, *El Alma Joven...* was gold-certified, selling more than 500,000 copies, and his song "**Querida**" was at the top of the Mexican charts for a whole year. He was inducted into the Billboard Latin Music Hall of Fame, the Latin Songwriters Hall of Fame, the International Latin Music Hall of Fame, and the Hollywood Walk of Fame.

Juan Gabriel never forgot his own childhood and strived to help children in similar situations, performing at benefit concerts and founding Semjase, a home for orphaned children. He said, *"I don't believe in competing, because there's room for everyone. You have to compete with yourself, because your duty to grow as a human being and keep your humility is much more important."*

# JULIA ALVAREZ

**DOMINICAN REPUBLIC**

**Julia Alvarez** is a Dominican-American poet, novelist, and essayist who has enchanted readers of all ages. Born in New York, Julia spent her early years in the Dominican Republic (DR) until her family fled due to her father's involvement in a rebellion against dictator Rafael Trujillo.

Julia's bestselling novel *How the García Girls Lost Their Accents* won the **PEN Oakland / Josephine Miles Literary Award**. The novel was influenced by her own challenges with prejudice after leaving the DR, and her feelings of homesickness and alienation, which is when people feel isolated from the society around them.

Her second novel, *In the Time of the Butterflies*, tells the incredible story of the Mirabal sisters and their struggle against Trujillo's dictatorship (see page 15). Julia's poetic side shines through in works like *Homecoming* and *The Woman I Kept to Myself*, and she shares her own life story in the autobiographical essays of *Something to Declare*.

She has crafted dozens of stories for younger readers, including the *Tía Lola* series and *Finding Miracles*, and she delves into the magical world of Dominican folklore in her picture book *The Secret Footprints*.

Being both Dominican and American, Julia's experiences of identity, immigration, and making a new place your home influence her writing. She has won a huge number of awards for her work, including the Hispanic Heritage Award in Literature and the National Medal of Arts from President Barack Obama.

Julia is also an activist, working hard to promote positive relations between Haiti and the DR. Step into Julia's world, where words have the power to bridge cultures and inspire change.

*Award-Winning Poet, Novelist, and Essayist*

# SYLVIA RIVERA

**(1951–2002)**

**Sylvia Rivera** was a Latine activist who campaigned for LGBTQ+ rights and paved the way for transgender equality.

Born in New York City to Venezuelan and Puero Rican parents, Sylvia faced immense challenges during her childhood. She was raised by her grandmother after her father left and her mother passed away. Sadly, her grandmother didn't accept her bisexual, transgender identity, leading to Sylvia running away from home at age 11. She was forced to live on the streets, but Sylvia persevered and turned her painful experiences into powerful motivation.

Sylvia always stood up for what she believed in, once describing herself as having "**revolutionary blood**." When she was just a teenager, she was involved in the Black Liberation Movement and the peace movement. Sylvia was also pivotal in the 1969 STONEWALL UPRISING, a historic protest against police that kickstarted the gay rights movement.

As a transgender woman, Sylvia recognized the exclusion of transgender individuals, especially those of color, from gay and lesbian communities, and she fought to challenge this injustice. Alongside her friend Marsha P. Johnson, Sylvia founded **STAR (Street Transvestite Action Revolutionaries)**. One of the first transgender advocacy groups in America, STAR became a vital space for addressing issues within the transgender community. Later in life, Sylvia advocated for the inclusion of transgender people in the **Sexual Orientation Non-Discrimination Act**, which passed into law in 2002. Sylvia's legacy lives on through **the Sylvia Rivera Law Project**, working to ensure that everyone can choose their gender identity, regardless of background or race, without facing discrimination.

In honor of Sylvia's impact, an intersection near the site of the Stonewall Uprising was renamed "**Sylvia Rivera Way**" and her portrait hangs in the National Portrait Gallery in Washington, D.C. Sylvia's courageous efforts continue to inspire positive change and acceptance for all.

U.S.A.

PUERTO RICO

VENEZUELA

## LGBTQ+ Trailblazer and Transgender Activist

# MARGARITA ENGLE

**(1951–PRESENT)**

Imagine a world where words bloom like flowers and stories dance like the wind. That's the world of Cuban-American poet and author, **Margarita Engle**. She is a writing wizard, with over 20 award-winning books for children, teens, and adults. Her books foster empathy, and are influenced by her Cuban heritage and appreciation of nature.

Margarita said that as a child, she *"was a shy bookworm with glasses, a long braid, a broken tooth, and homemade mother-daughter clothes. I loved plants and animals, especially horses. I wrote poetry."*

Margarita was born and raised in her father's hometown, Los Angeles, but she spent her summers in Cuba. There, she developed a deep bond with her extended family and a lifelong passion for tropical nature. This led to her studying botany and working as an agronomy professor, an irrigation water-conservation specialist, and a scientific writer, before writing books for children.

In recognition of her fantastic talent, Margarita was made the **Young People's Poet Laureate** from 2017 to 2019. In this role, she shared her poetry, put on workshops, and engaged with kids and teens at schools, libraries, and literary events

to encourage their interest in poetry and literature.

Margarita has won dozens of awards, including **Pura Belpré Awards**. She was the first Latine person to win a special award called the Newbery Honor for her book *The Surrender Tree: Poems of Cuba's Struggle for Freedom*: a lyrical novel in verse about Cuba and one of the country's national heroes (and feminist icons), Rosa Castellanos.

Margarita creates enchanting stories that make you laugh, cry, and think. So, if you ever pick up one of her books, get ready for a journey into a world of wonder and imagination!

U.S.A.

*The Magical Wordsmith*

# MICHELLE BACHELET

(1951–PRESENT)

**First Female President in South America**

CHILE

Verónica Michelle Bachelet Jeria is a Chilean leader who has dedicated her life to making a positive impact on her country and the world. She was the **United Nations High Commissioner for Human Rights**, as well as the first elected female president in South America.

Born in Chile to a military family, Michelle spent her childhood moving between military bases in her home country and the United States. She was a busy student, joining volleyball teams and theater groups, and even becoming class president.

In 1973, Michelle's father was taken prisoner during the rule of General Pinochet, an army officer who overthrew the government. Her father sadly died, and Michelle and her mother were also held as prisoners and interrogated. Fortunately, Michelle found refuge in Australia and Germany, where she studied medicine. When she returned to Chile, her qualifications were not recognized, so she re-enrolled at university and graduated as a surgeon.

Michelle consulted for the Pan-American Health Organization and the World Health Organization, before becoming Chile's Minister of Health. She successfully reduced public hospital waiting lists by 90%. She also studied military strategy and became the Minister of National Defense, the first woman in Latin America to do so.

Continuing to break barriers, she became the first female president of Chile in 2006, championing healthcare and electoral reforms. She launched educational programs emphasizing social justice, including the delivery of free books to thousands of underprivileged families. She also introduced laws and maternity packages to challenge gender inequality. She was the **first Chilean president** to be elected to a second term since 1932.

Michelle's story highlights how resilience, determination, and compassionate leadership can create positive change in the world.

# BERNARDO GUARACHI

**Pro Mountain Climber**

BOLIVIA

**Bernardo Guarachi Mamani** is a Bolivian mountain climber and guide. In 1998, he became the first Latin American to climb Mount Everest: the highest mountain in the world with an altitude of **29,032 ft**.

Bernardo was born in Bolivia, but was adopted at the age of seven and grew up in Arica, Chile. He later returned to his home country, driven by his passion for climbing and his desire to reach the peak of Illimani, the second highest mountain in Bolivia. Bernardo successfully climbed Illimani not just once, but **170 times!**

On January 9, 2020, he completed the Seven Summits, a challenge where mountaineers climb seven of the highest mountains on the seven continents.

Bernardo climbed:
1. **Mount Everest in Asia (29,032 ft)**
2. **Aconcagua in South America (22,838 ft)**
3. **Denali in North America (20,310 ft)**
4. **Mount Kilimanjaro in Africa (19,341 ft)**
5. **Mount Elbrus in Europe (18,510 ft)**
6. **Vinson Massif in Antarctica (16,050 ft)**
7. **Puncak Jaya (AKA Carstensz Pyramid) in Oceania (16,024 ft).**

Climbing runs in the family, as Bernardo's son, Eliot, is also a talented mountaineer. Bernardo and Eliot were the first two Bolivians to ascend Cho Oyu, a mountain in the Himalayas with an altitude of 26,906 ft.

Bernardo's adventurous spirit, his bravery, and his love of climbing have made him a true mountain hero, both in Bolivia and around the world, and he continues to inspire others to reach new heights.

**Sonia Maria Sotomayor** was born in the Bronx, New York City. She is a distinguished legal scholar, trailblazing jurist, author, and the first Latina **Supreme Court Justice**. Justice Sotomayor's remarkable journey started with a modest upbringing in city-owned housing projects. Her Puerto Rican parents worked hard to provide for her and her brother. Her mother was a telephone operator and nurse. Her father worked in a factory. Despite facing challenges like poverty, diabetes, and the death of her father when she was nine, Sonia was dedicated to achieving her dreams. She was the valedictorian of her high school graduating class, then graduated *summa cum laude* (highest honours) from Princeton

University before earning her Juris Doctor from **Yale Law School**.

Throughout her law career, Sonia has championed the rights of marginalized communities. When she makes legal decisions, she thinks about the impact on real Americans. Many commend her for being an empathetic judge, which means she always tries to understand what other people feel by imagining herself in their place. She is celebrated for advocating for civil rights protection, criminal justice reform, and access to education.

Sonia is an inspirational figure beyond the courtroom, too. She uses her platform to inspire young people, particularly those

from underrepresented backgrounds, to pursue education and careers in law. She said, "*There are uses to adversity, and they don't reveal themselves until tested. Whether it's serious illness, financial hardship, or the simple constraint of parents who speak limited English, difficulty can tap unexpected strengths.*"

Sonia's legacy is one of intellect, resilience, and a profound commitment to justice. Her role in shaping the nation's legal landscape makes her a beacon of hope for those who believe in equality, fairness, and the power of the law to create positive change.

# SONIA SOTOMAYOR

(1954–PRESENT)

U.S.A.

SEAL OF THE SUPREME COURT OF THE UNITED STATES

*First Latina Supreme Court Justice*

**Gloria Estefan** is a sensational Cuban-American singer, actor, and businesswoman who has captured the hearts of fans worldwide.

Born Gloria María Milagrosa Fajardo García in Havana, Cuba, Gloria was just two years old when her family fled to Miami, Florida, during the Cuban Revolution. Growing up, she helped to run her family's Cuban restaurant. Life took a challenging turn when her father fell ill after serving in the Vietnam War, and Gloria became one of his caregivers. When times were hard, she found escape and joy in music. Little did she know that this would lead her to stardom!

Discovered by the manager of a band called Miami Sound Machine (formerly Miami Latin Boys), Gloria became their lead singer and they earned worldwide success with the song "*Conga*."

Things were not always easy. In 1990, a traffic accident left Gloria with a life-threatening spine fracture. Fortunately, she made an amazing recovery through determination, therapy, and unwavering support from those around her. Gloria showcased her incredible resilience by launching a comeback album, *Into the Light*, just one year after the accident.

With EIGHT Grammy Awards and the esteemed Presidential Medal of Freedom, Gloria is considered one of the most successful artists ever. Her record sales have exceeded 100 million copies worldwide and she's had 38 number one hits across Billboard charts, including "**Don't Wanna Lose You**," "**Turn the Beat Around**," and "**Get on Your Feet**."

Gloria has been recognized with a Hollywood Walk of Fame star, a **Lifetime Achievement Award** from the American Music Awards, and inclusion in the Songwriters Hall of Fame. She is a true icon, proving that with passion and perseverance, you can be unstoppable.

(1957–PRESENT)

GLORIA ESTEFAN

CUBA

*Singer, Actor, and Icon*

# ELLEN OCHOA

(1958– PRESENT)

**Ellen Lauri Ochoa** is a Mexican-American engineer and astronaut. She made history as the first Latina to go to space!

Her story begins in California, where she was born. She was the valedictorian at her high school and at San Diego State University, where she graduated with a bachelor's degree in physics. She then pursued a master's and doctorate in **electrical engineering** from Stanford University.

Ellen applied to be a NASA astronaut many times and was rejected—but that didn't stop her. She took a job as a research engineer until she was selected to be an astronaut. Her first mission aboard the space shuttle *Discovery* studied the Earth's ozone layer for nine days.

Ellen has flown into space FOUR times, totaling about 1,000 hours in orbit. On her flights, her roles ranged from robotic arm operator to payload commander, which means she planned, managed, and conducted scientific activities in space. She also served as a flight engineer, ensuring the spacecraft functioned safely and correctly. Ochoa is also an award-winning flutist, and she took a flute on her first mission to space.

She is in the U.S. Astronaut Hall of Fame, the International Air & Space Hall of Fame, and the California Hall of Fame. Ellen has earned many awards, like the **Distinguished Service Medal**, which is NASA's highest award. She received the Presidential Distinguished Rank Award for senior executives in the federal government after her appointment as the 11th director of the Johnson Space Center. She was the first Latine and the second female director.

She also has eight honorary doctorates and is proud to have six schools named after her. She said, *"Education is what allows you to stand out. It was the key to my selection as an astronaut, and continuing to learn at every step of the way has brought me to new heights."*

MEXICO

NASA

NASA

**Engineer and First Latina in Space!**

# EVELYN CISNEROS

**(1958–PRESENT)**

U.S.A.

MEXICO

## The Prima Ballerina Who Danced into History!

Get ready to twirl into the world of **Evelyn Cisneros**, the trailblazing ballerina who danced her way into history as the first Latina prima ballerina in the United States!

Growing up, Evelyn was very shy, so her mother enrolled her in dance class. She found her footing and place in the dazzling world of ballet. However, it took a lot of work for Evelyn. Her left hip was too tight and her left foot was pigeon-toed. She also faced discrimination, and was told to paint her neck, chest, arms, and face with makeup to lighten her dark skin. Despite these challenges,

her strong work ethic enabled her to soar in the ballet universe.

She joined the San Francisco Ballet Company and danced with them for 23 years. A remarkable talent, she performed nearly every starring role in their collection. She danced her heart out as Princess Aurora in "*Sleeping Beauty*," twirled like magic as the Sugar Plum Fairy in "*The Nutcracker*," and brought tears of joy and sorrow as Odette in "*Swan Lake*."

After retiring as a dancer, Evelyn became a teacher and continued to

inspire new generations of dancers of all backgrounds to follow their passion. She taught at the Boston Ballet School, New York City Ballet, Pacific Northwest Ballet, Ballet Florida, State Theatre Ballet in South Africa, and Northern Ballet Theatre in England. She also holds honorary doctorates from Mills College and the University of California.

Evelyn's legacy is one of shattering barriers. In a world where ballerinas of Mexican and Latinx heritage are rare, she proved with every pirouette that dreams know no bounds.

# RIGOBERTA MENCHÚ

(1959–PRESENT)

Meet **Rigoberta Menchú Tum**, a remarkable Guatemalan activist dedicated to fighting for the rights of Indigenous peoples in her homeland. Rigoberta's journey began as a child. She worked alongside her poor Mayan family and experienced first hand the hardships faced by impoverished farm workers, which ignited a fire within her to stand up for those in need.

Rigoberta joined social reform activities advocating for women and poor laborers. Her courage in pursuing social justice brought her face-to-face with opposition. Accusations of the family's involvement in rebellion led to her father's imprisonment and torture.

After his release, he joined **the Committee of the Peasant Union (CUC)**, and Rigoberta followed suit. But tragedy struck when her brother, father, and mother were arrested, tortured, and tragically killed by the Guatemalan army. Despite her profound grief, Rigoberta organized strikes to improve farmworker conditions. She also educated Mayans on resisting military oppression.

Persistent death threats forced her into exile. She went into hiding in Guatemala before seeking refuge in Mexico. Her resilience led her to return to Guatemala multiple times, but her life was in danger.

From abroad, Rigoberta played a vital role in establishing **the United Representation of the Guatemalan Opposition (RUOG)**, working to resist oppression in Guatemala. She also became a member of the **National Coordinating Committee of the CUC**.

Today, Rigoberta Menchú is a leading advocate for Indigenous rights in Guatemala and the Western Hemisphere. Her unwavering commitment earned her numerous international accolades, including the prestigious NOBEL PEACE PRIZE in 1992. Rigoberta's story reminds us all that we can make the world a better place.

GUATEMALA

*Indigenous Rights Activist*

# GUILLERMO DEL TORO

## Award-Winning Filmmaker and Spooky Storyteller

MEXICO

**Guillermo del Toro Gómez** is a filmmaker, author, and makeup artist from Mexico. He brings monsters and fairy tales to life through his movies and books, using his skills to find beauty in the scary and strange.

Growing up in a strict Catholic home, he found his passion for storytelling at a young age. He started to make short films when he was only eight years old, using his toys and his father's camera. Guillermo's imagination soared as he studied filmmaking at the University of Guadalajara. At this time, he also wrote a book about his hero: the film director, screenwriter, producer, and editor Alfred Hitchcock.

Guillermo has worked on many famous movies, including *Pan's Labyrinth*, *The Shape of Water*, *The Book of Life*, and *The Hobbit* films, where he brings monsters, magic, and fantasy worlds to the big screen. He has also created animated series for television, including *Trollhunters*.

But his creativity doesn't stop there. Guillermo has written and co-written several books—often horror stories with a cast of spooky characters.

Guillermo has won THREE Academy Awards and THREE British Academy Film Awards, and his impact on the world of cinema earned him a star on the **Hollywood Walk of Fame**.

Guillermo is not just a filmmaker, he's a monster enthusiast, a storyteller extraordinaire, and someone who finds wonder in all things weird.

**(1966–PRESENT)**

MEXICO

U.S.A.

*Actor, Producer, and Hollywood Megastar*

# SALMA HAYEK

**Salma Hayek** is a Mexican-American actor and film producer. Born Salma Valgarma Hayek Jiménez, she started her career in Mexico, dazzling audiences with her talent in telenovelas, before making a big splash in Hollywood.

As a child, Salma loved being on stage, and she worked hard to get to where she wanted to be. When she was at school, she was diagnosed with dyslexia, a learning difference that can make reading and writing difficult. Although this presented challenges for Salma, she persevered and didn't let anything stand in her way to becoming a star.

Her breakout role in the film *Desperado* showcased Salma as the self-confident and feisty Carolina, earning her an American Latino Media Arts Award nomination. She later went on to make history with her portrayal of painter Frida Kahlo (see page 13) in the biopic *Frida*, becoming the FIRST MEXICAN actor to be nominated for the Academy Award for Best Actress. This last role also earned her a Golden Globe Award and a Screen Actors Guild Award. Salma then turned her focus to producing. She produced and starred in *In the Time of the Butterflies*, a film based on Julia Alvarez's (see page 31) book telling the amazing story of the Mirabal sisters (see page 15). She also served as an executive producer for the Golden Globe-winning series *Ugly Betty*.

Salma is the CEO of her own Latin film production company, Ventanarosa. She signed a deal with ABC to develop projects, and uses her position to create opportunities for Latine actors looking for stardom. Her directing, producing, and acting work on television has earned her multiple Emmy Awards.

Salma Hayek's journey teaches us to pursue our dreams relentlessly. Anything is possible with talent, determination, and a bit of flair!

# MARIANO RIVERA

(1969–PRESENT)

PANAMÁ

U.S.A.

## Record-Breaking Baseball Legend

**Mariano Rivera** is a Panamanian-American superstar baseball player. He is known for throwing pitches at more than **90 miles per hour**—so fast that they often broke bats!

Growing up in a fishing village in Panama, Mariano's favorite sport was soccer and his favorite player was the Brazilian superstar Pelé. Sadly, Mariano had to quit soccer after several ankle and knee injuries, but his love of baseball grew. His early baseball days involved cardboard gloves, tree branch bats, and makeshift balls created from taped-up fishing nets.

In ninth grade, Mariano dropped out of school to work in the fishing trade, but he continued playing baseball as a hobby whenever he could. He was finally scouted and signed by the Yankees in 1990. Mariano's determination and talent prevailed over challenges including language barriers and elbow surgery. He played an incredible 19 seasons for the New York Yankees, with a record-breaking 1,173 strikeouts, and he helped the team win multiple World Series titles.

His legendary career has so many highlights, including being a **13-time All-Star** (best player), a **five-time World Series champion**, and the

**all-time leader** in saves (652) and games finished (952) in Major League Baseball. He was the 1999 World Series Most Valuable Player and he made history as the first player elected unanimously into the Baseball Hall of Fame.

Off the field, Mariano is committed to helping disadvantaged children reach their potential, and he received the Presidential Medal of Freedom for his charity work. He once said, *"I would love to be remembered as a player who was always there for others."* And indeed he is, being recognized as a baseball hero, a symbol of perseverance, and a philanthropic champion.

Selena Quintanilla-Pérez was a Mexican-American singer and fashion trendsetter. She propelled Tejano music (a style that mixes Mexican and American influences) into the mainstream, becoming known as the "*Queen of Tejano*."

Born in Texas, Selena's musical journey began at age six, when her father noticed her incredible talent. At age nine, she started singing in a family band, **Selena y Los Dinos**, performing at shows, weddings, and parties to help her family make money. As the success of the band grew, it was hard for Selena to balance performing and schoolwork. She was also criticized for performing Tejano music because it was usually performed by men. But she persevered and her popularity began to soar.

In 1989, Selena signed a deal with a record company and released many successful albums, including ***Entre a Mi Mundo*** which held the number one spot on the Billboard chart for eight months in a row. She is considered one of the greatest Latine artists of all time, with over **18 MILLION** records sold worldwide. She also had an amazing sense of style, designing her own successful clothing line and opening fashion stores.

Tragically, Selena's life was cut short when she was killed in 1995 by a woman who worked for her. Selena's latest album, ***Dreaming of You***, was released after her death and became a record-breaking success, with five million copies sold. A film about Selena's incredible life and career was later released to share her story with fans around the world.

Selena was a trailblazer who helped redefine Latin music. She elevated styles including Tejano, cumbia, and Latin pop. Selena's success opened doors for other Latine musicians, and her legacy lives on through her timeless music and her cultural impact.

SELENA

(1971–1995)

MEXICO

**Music and Style Icon**

# FRANCISCO RUBIO

## (1975–PRESENT)

U.S.A.

EL SALVADOR

### Astronaut, Pilot, and Flight Surgeon

Ready for blast-off? Launch yourself into the incredible world of **Francisco Rubio**, an El Salvadorian-American army lieutenant, helicopter pilot, flight surgeon, and NASA astronaut.

Born in the United States, Francisco spent his early years in El Salvador, before moving with his family to Miami, Florida, when he was six years old. While in the military, Francisco discovered his love of flying and began his career as a pilot. He flew a UH-60 Black Hawk helicopter, totaling over 1,100 hours of flying time, including 600 mission hours in countries such as Bosnia, Iraq, and Afghanistan. He was a member of renowned parachute team the "**Black Knights**," and he earned the title "**Jumpmaster**," having completed over 650 freefall skydives.

As well as his passion for flying, Francisco had dreams of becoming a doctor. Deciding to make his ambitions a reality, he studied at the Uniformed Services University of the Health Sciences, and went on to serve as a clinic supervisor and flight surgeon.

As if being a pilot and a doctor wasn't impressive enough, Francisco went one step further and became an astronaut! He launched aboard the Soyuz MS-22 spacecraft on September 21, 2022, on a six-month mission to the International Space Station. The journey ended up lasting more than a year due to a damaged spacecraft. When Francisco returned to Earth, he had set the record for the **longest spaceflight** by an American astronaut, lasting 371 days. He also conducted three spacewalks, totaling 21 hours and 24 minutes.

Francisco has received many awards and badges, including the Meritorious Service Medal and the Army Achievement Medal. Francisco's story shows that with ambition and hard work, even the sky isn't the limit!

**Luis von Ahn** is a Guatemalan computer scientist, entrepreneur, and academic professor. He is of German-Jewish descent, but was born and raised in Guatemala before moving to the United States. Both of Luis' parents were doctors, so he grew up in a prosperous household and attended the prestigious American School of Guatemala. When he was eight, his mom bought him a **Commodore 64** computer, and this sparked his lifelong fixation with technology.

Luis studied Mathematics at Duke University and went on to earn his Ph.D. in Computer Science from Carnegie Mellon University, where he now serves as an associate professor. He believes that learning should always be fun, just like playing video games or using social media apps.

During his impressive career, Luis developed a learning app called **Duolingo**, which helps people learn new languages. He also created the internet security tool **reCAPTCHA**, which is used to prove that web users are human and not automated robots. ReCAPTCHA has been hugely popular, with over 100,000 websites making use of it.

Luis earned the Presidential Early Career Award for Scientists and Engineers, as well as the Lemelson-MIT Prize, which recognizes young inventors and their technology-based ideas. He has appeared on numerous lists celebrating his achievements, including being named one of the "**50 Best Brains in Science**" by *Discover* magazine.

In 2021, Luis established the **Luis von Ahn Foundation**, which works to improve the rights of women and girls in Guatemala, promoting equality and social justice and creating an environment ready for progress of all kinds. Luis' love for technology at a young age reminds us that our interests are important and can lead to incredible success in the future.

# LUIS VON AHN

## (1978–PRESENT)

GUATEMALA

*Computer Scientist and Entrepreneur*

# LIN-MANUEL MIRANDA

## (1980–PRESENT)

## Award-Winning Creative Genius

**Lin-Manuel Miranda** is a man of many talents: He is a songwriter, an actor, a director, a producer, and an author. Born in New York City to Puerto Rican (PR) parents, he is the brilliant mind behind multiple award-winning works, including musicals and movie soundtracks. Even though he grew up in Washington Heights, NYC, he spent most of his summers in Puerto Rico with his grandparents, which is where his PR pride took root.

He was in the drama club in high school before graduating and studying theater at Wesleyan University, which was where he wrote the first draft of *In the Heights*—the musical that put him on the map due to the catchy music and relatable characters. It is a love letter to his home—Washington Heights in Manhattan—and it was a huge success, winning **FOUR** Tony Awards (including Best Musical and Best Score), a Grammy, and a nomination for the Pulitzer Prize for Drama.

Lin-Manuel's most famous work, *Hamilton*, hit Broadway in 2015. An original musical that draws on hip-hop and rap to tell the story of Founding Father Alexander Hamilton, the show featured a racially diverse cast and made U.S. history feel accessible worldwide. It blew audiences away and earned many high-profile awards, including the Pulitzer Prize for Drama and a record-breaking **11** Tony Awards.

Lin-Manuel is also famous for creating renowned movie soundtracks. He collaborated with Disney to produce the original song "**How Far I'll Go**" for the movie *Moana*, earning him an Academy Award nomination and a Grammy. All eight of the original songs he wrote for the film *Encanto* appeared on the Billboard "HOT 100" in the same week, with "**We Don't Talk About Bruno**" sticking at number one for five weeks and "**Dos Oruguitas**" receiving an Academy nomination.

He directed his first film, *tick, tick... BOOM!*, in 2021, based on playwright Jonathan Larson's struggle to navigate his career, love, and friendship. The film received several awards and Lin-Manuel was named Best Director by the Detroit Film Critics Association. Lin-Manuel has been recognized with a huge number of awards and has stars on the **Walks of Fame** in both Hollywood and Puerto Rico. He is determined to use his success to help others, and he actively speaks out about causes that are important to him, including Puerto Rico's financial security, equality for people of color, and women's reproductive health. He also founded 5000 Broadway Productions to uplift diverse voices in the arts.

Lin-Manuel is an icon in the world of arts and entertainment, and his story shows how important it is to embrace your talents and share them with the world.

# FRANCIA MÁRQUEZ

## Fearless Environmental and Human Rights Activist

COLOMBIA

(1981–PRESENT)

**Francia Elena Márquez Mina** is an Afro-Colombian human rights and environmental activist. A lawyer by trade, she was the 13TH vice president of Colombia. After taking office, Francia became the first Afro-Colombian vice president in the country's history and only the second woman to hold the post. She first became an activist aged 13, protesting the construction of a dam that threatened her community.

She became a local leader at a young age, using Afro-Colombian music and dance to advocate for her environment and ancestral land.

Her home, La Toma, is also home to a quarter million Afro-Colombians: the "**descendants of free people who were enslaved**" from Africa, who rely on the Ovejas River for clean drinking water and fish. Thousands of illegal miners began clearing forests, digging deep open pits, and using toxic chemicals, like mercury and cyanide, to extract gold. They contaminated the water.

Francia did not stand by. She spoke powerfully about the legacy of her community and how that history inspires her, saying, "*Each generation of my community has been in a constant struggle—for survival, for freedom, for the land.*"

She organized her community to fight against multinational mining companies and educated farmers on sustainable agricultural techniques. Francia spearheaded a 10-day, 350-mile march of 80 women to the nation's capital. Once in Bogota, Francia and the women spent 22 DAYS protesting on the streets, resulting in the eradication of illegal mining. As a result of Francia's work, all illegal miners and their equipment were removed from her community's ancestral land. The government also created the first national task force on illegal mining.

After this victory, Francia became Vice President even though some people said scary things to try to hurt and threaten her. She shows us all that there is power in numbers and that protesting can bring about change for the world and the environment. Francia is a fearless example of using your voice to speak up for what you believe in.

Meet **Diana Lorena Taurasi**, the incredible basketball star who has left her mark on the game! Her father was a huge influence on her. He was a professional soccer player and encouraged her to be proud of her Argentine roots by speaking Spanish in their California home. She is among history's top 15 Women's National Basketball Association (WNBA) players. The legendary Kobe Bryant called her *"The White Mamba,"* comparing Diana to himself. Standing tall at 6 feet, she's a basketball legend and a proud owner of a dog named Messi.

While playing for the University of Connecticut, Diana was Player of the Year THREE TIMES. She led them to three national titles, and had a 70-game win streak. She then took the WNBA by storm as Rookie of the Year before becoming a WNBA All-Decade team member after only two seasons. Diana is a seven-time All-Star, a three-time WNBA champion, a record-holding nine-time All-WNBA First Team selection, and the 2009 WNBA MVP.

Diana also dominates internationally. She has won four straight Euroleague championships and was named **European Player of the Year** for three seasons. She even led her team to Olympic gold in Beijing, London, and Athens.

Off the court, Diana is known for her kindness. She signs autographs for everyone, including opposing team fans. She is incredibly humble, saying, *"Who's to say Michael Jordan is better than Oscar Robertson or Magic Johnson or Larry Bird? Every generation has its great players. There's never going to be one player that's so above and beyond anyone else."* Her discipline in the gym and dedication to her health shows the work ethic she learned from her dad.

Diana Taurasi isn't just a basketball player; she's a game-changer, inspiring kids and fans worldwide. Whether making incredible shots or spreading positivity, Diana is a true superstar on and off the court!

Basketball Player and the "White Mamba"

ARGENTINA

30 : 20

#1

WNBA

DIANA TAURASI

(1982–PRESENT)

# SOFÍA MULÁNOVICH

(1983–PRESENT)

Meet **Sofía Mulánovich Aljovín**, the incredible three-time world surfing champion from Peru! She's the first Latin American to win a World Surf League (WSL) Championship Tour event. But that's not all—Sofía is the only Latina athlete to win **TWO International Surfing Association (ISA) World Championships**.

Her passion for surfing started when she was three. Her father worked at a fish-processing plant, and surfed with Sofía and her brothers in his time off. At age 13, she competed in the U.S. Open of Surfing competition and made it to the quarter-finals.

Now she is a record-breaker, having triumphed in prestigious competitions like **the Vans Triple Crown of Surfing**, **the U.S. Open of Surfing**, and **the Surfer Poll**. Sofía's outstanding achievements earned her induction into the **Surfing Hall of Fame**, which is like a special club for the best surfers in the world.

But Sofía isn't just about breaking records in the water. She's a champion on land, too. She started a surfing academy to teach kids from all backgrounds how to surf. She said, *"When I was a little kid, I used to dream about this. I've done this for my country and for all South Americans."*

A hero for the LGBTQ+ community, Sofía is openly lesbian and has welcomed a son with her girlfriend, Camila Toro. She's shown all young Latina athletes that they can achieve their dreams, no matter how big they are.

Sofía Mulánovich is a fantastic athlete and an excellent role model for being true to yourself. She is a surfing sensation and a champion for all. Surf's up, Sofía!

*The Surfing Superstar*

# MARTA VIEIRA DA SILVA

**(1986–PRESENT)**

## Record-Setting Soccer Player

**Marta Vieira da Silva** is a Brazilian-Swedish soccer player who has taken the football world by storm. She plays for the Orlando Pride in the National Women's Soccer League in the United States, as well as playing for the national team of Brazil. Marta is considered one of the greatest footballers of all time.

Marta's story began in Dios Riachos, a small town in Brazil, where she was raised by her mother. Marta was the only girl in the area who played soccer, and she was excluded from games by her male peers. Only a few years prior, it had been illegal for girls to play soccer in Brazil, a ban that wasn't lifted until 1979! Undeterred, Marta played soccer in any way she could, even kicking balls made of grocery bags through the streets. She was eventually allowed on a boys' junior team and, at the age of 14, she was scouted.

Marta's career soared. She won numerous championships, including the UEFA (Union of European Football Associations) Women's Cup and seven Swedish league titles.

Marta went on to set some incredible soccer records:

- Brazil's top goal scorer of any gender (115 goals)
- Most goals at the World Cup level (17 goals)
- First footballer of any gender to score at five different World Cups
- Scoring at five Olympic Games in a row

Marta is a SIX-TIME winner of the FIFA (International Federation of Association Football) World Player of the Year award. She earned both the Golden Ball (for best player) and the Golden Boot (for top scorer) in the 2007 Women's World Cup. She is a true inspiration, refusing to give up on her dreams and talent, and breaking barriers for aspiring athletes everywhere.

# ROMÁN GONZÁLEZ

**(1987–PRESENT)**

NICARAGUA

## TEIKEN

### The Boxing Icon Who Defied the Odds!

**Román Alberto González Luna** is a boxing legend from Nicaragua, best known by his nickname "*Chocolatito.*" Román is the first boxer from Nicaragua to win world titles in four weight classes. He surpassed his mentor and former three-weight world champion, the late Alexis Argüello.

You must be wondering how he got his nickname . . . when he was about 14 years old, Román met Alexis Argüello and trained at his gym. Román's father was also a boxer known as Chocolate because of the color of his skin. As a result, Alexis Argüello gave Román the nickname "Chocolatito," which means "little chocolate."

At just **18** years old, Román turned pro in the Minimumweight/Light Flyweight division. He won **EIGHT** fights in a row by knockout! He didn't stop there. Román held **the World Boxing Association (WBA)** Minimumweight title, the WBA Light Flyweight title, the WBA Super Flyweight title, and the **World Boxing Council** Super Flyweight title.

Román was ranked by **ESPN** as the world's best active boxer, pound for pound. He is known mainly for his aggressive pressure-fighting style. Out of 55 fights, Román won a whopping **51 times**, with an incredible **41 knockouts**!

It's important to know that Román's story isn't just about punching gloves and winning belts. He's a real-life superhero for young dreamers everywhere. He wants them to know that "*no matter where you are from and what economical situation you find yourself in, if your heart desires to be great, you can achieve it . . .*" He's a true inspiration, proving that anyone can reach for those championship belts with determination!

(1987–PRESENT)

**Lionel Andrés Messi** is an **Argentine** professional soccer player who plays as a forward and team captain. He is widely regarded as one of the greatest players of all time. At age four, his father, a steel factory manager, coached him. But his biggest influence was his **abuela (grandmother)**, who took him to training and matches. He honors his abuela by looking up and pointing to the sky after a goal.

Messi has played for Barcelona, Argentina, and Inter Miami. He has won a record **EIGHT** **Ballon d'Or awards** (given to the best soccer player in the world). He also won **SIX** **European Golden Shoes**—an award presented to the leading goalscorer in the European national league.

He broke records by winning **THIRTY-FOUR** trophies, **SEVEN** Copa del Rey titles, the UEFA Champions League four times, the Copa América, and the 2022 FIFA World Cup. He holds the records for most goals (474), the most assists (192), the most hat-tricks (36), and the most international goals by a South American male (106). Messi was among *Time* magazine's 100 most influential people worldwide in **2011**, **2012**, and **2023**.

We should all strive to reach our goals like Messi. His future as a professional player was threatened at age 10 when he was diagnosed with a growth hormone deficiency, but he did not let this stop him, and now he makes his abuela proud with every goal.

## Record-Breaking and World-Renowned Soccer Player

# ALEXANDRIA OCASIO-CORTEZ

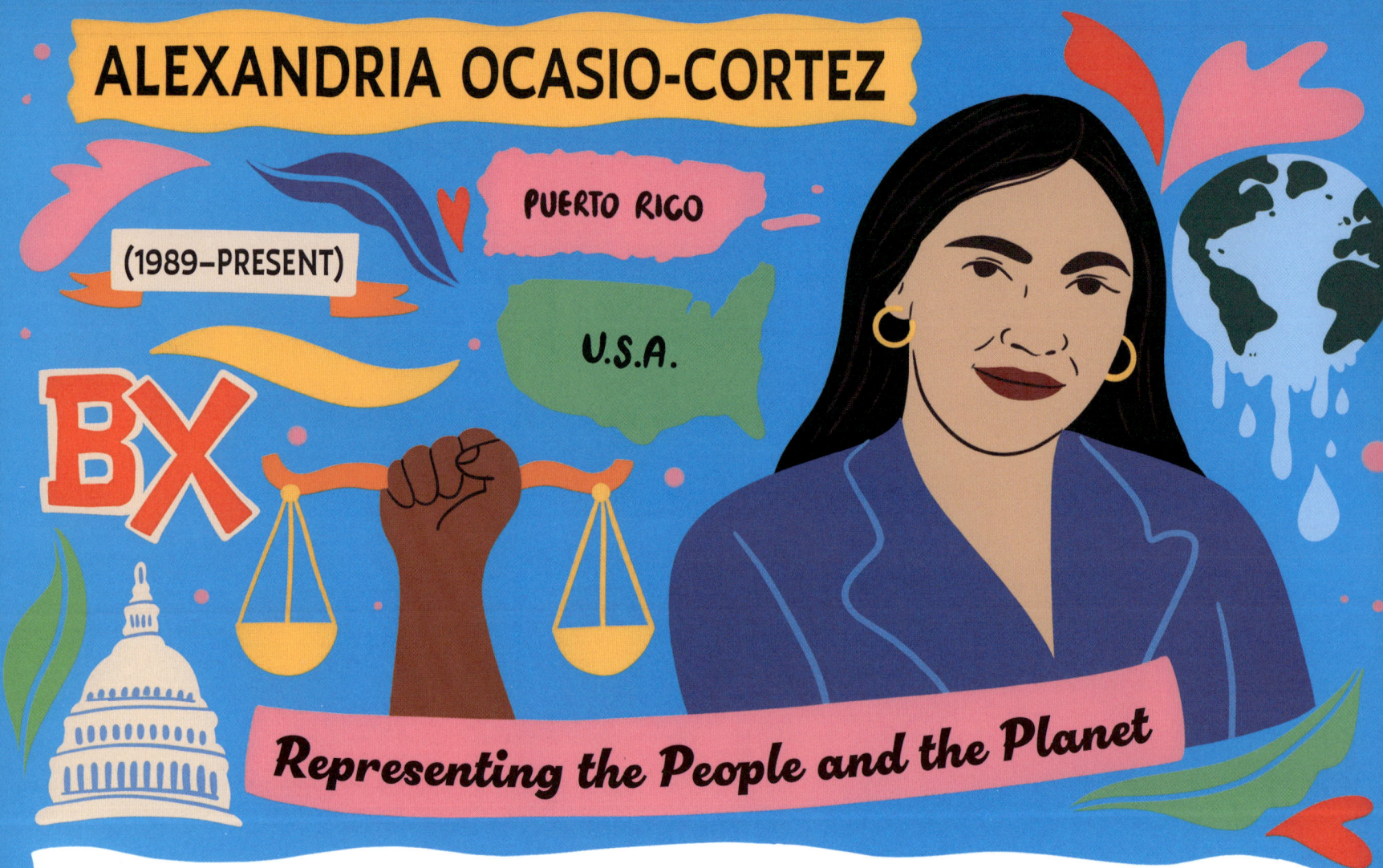

(1989–PRESENT)

PUERTO RICO

U.S.A.

BX

## Representing the People and the Planet

Puerto Rican-American **Alexandria Ocasio-Cortez (AOC)** made history when she became the youngest woman and the youngest Latina to serve in the United States Congress.

Born in The Bronx, New York, her family moved to the Yorktown suburbs when she was five years old. Alexandria studied **Economics and International Relations** at Boston University. After graduating, she worked as the Educational Director at the National Hispanic Institute, supporting people from all walks of life to prepare them for a college education.

Sadly, Alexandria's life took an unexpected turn when her father died in 2008. The family almost lost their home because of expensive medical bills. Alexandria moved back to The Bronx and worked as a waitress and bartender to help her mother.

Driven by a deep concern for the struggles of everyday people, Alexandria was resolute in her mission to bring about positive changes to her city. In 2018, she launched her campaign to enter Congress and, against all odds, emerged victorious at the age of 29, making history as the youngest woman to do so. Her commitment to social justice is truly admirable.

Alexandria's passion for supporting young people and addressing climate change is a beacon of hope. During her first term in office, she secured an impressive $470 MILLION in grants for youth educational projects and green jobs training. She introduced the visionary "**Green New Deal**," a comprehensive set of laws aimed at creating millions of environmentally friendly jobs. Her efforts to make life-saving medications affordable and her relentless fight for financial support for those in need are testament to her dedication.

Alexandria Ocasio-Cortez's resilience and commitment to people and the environment show us that anyone, no matter their age, can shape a better future for all.

Meet **Verónica Cepede Royg**, the incredible tennis star from Paraguay who has conquered the courts with her powerful and explosive playing style.

Verónica's tennis journey started when she was just **FIVE** years old, thanks to her brother and sister introducing her to the courts. She grew up surrounded by tennis, aspiring to be like her idols Roger Federer and Kim Clijsters.

A formidable presence on the court, Verónica is an aggressive baseliner with a lethal forehand (her signature shot). Despite her 5-foot-4 stature—a factor many believed would be a hindrance—she defied expectations, and her powerful legs allowed her to cover the full court with ease.

Verónica has made her mark on the sport. She won a doubles title on the Women's Tennis Association (WTA) Tour and a WTA 125 **doubles championship**. She's won an amazing **14** International Tennis Federation **singles titles**.

Tennis has taken Verónica all over the world. She competed in the 2012 London Olympics, the 2016 Rio Olympics, the 2020 Tokyo Olympics, and the 2017 French Open.

Veronica has since retired from tennis but continues to exercise and eat healthily, knowing how important it is to keep her body strong and happy. If not for her tennis career, she would have likely ventured into the field of nutrition. In her leisure time, she also enjoys going to the movies with her family and friends.

Verónica Cepede Royg's story is one of determination, skill, and the joy of pursuing your passions, both on and off the court.

# VERÓNICA CEPEDE ROYG

(1992–PRESENT)

PARAGUAY

*Tennis Player Extraordinaire*

Sabrina Gonzalez Pasterski is a Cuban-American physicist who studies black holes and spacetime. Harvard University has called her the **next Albert Einstein**, and it's easy to see why!

Sabrina is a proud graduate of Chicago public schools. She credits her father for encouraging her to follow her dreams, one of which was to learn to fly. She started taking lessons at just 9 years old, and her first U.S. solo flight, when she was 14 years old, was on an aircraft that she had built herself!

She graduated from Massachusetts Institute of Technology (MIT) with a 5.0 GPA when she was 19, earning an award for her incredibly high grades. At MIT, she worked on a science experiment at the Large Hadron Collider (a giant machine that helps scientists understand tiny particles). The experiment explored dark matter and the possibility of other dimensions. She then completed her Ph.D. at Harvard University at age 25, discovering the "**spin memory effect**," which helps us learn more about waves in space, called **gravitational waves**, and their effects.

Many famous scientists, including Stephen Hawking and Andrew Strominger, have recognized Sabrina and built on her ideas in their work. When she was **27**, she started the Celestial Holography Initiative, bringing together a team of mathematicians, physicists, and computer scientists to share ideas about space using holograms. She has received many awards and grants for her fantastic research about our universe.

Sabrina is committed to getting more women and girls into the world of science. She promoted Michelle Obama's "**Let Girls Learn**" campaign and was invited to the White House in recognition of her support.

Sabrina Gonzalez Pasterski is a superhero scientist following her passions and working to unlock the universe's secrets!

# SABRINA GONZALEZ PASTERSKI

(1993–PRESENT)

U.S.A.

CUBA

**Space Scientist and Physics Phenomenon**

Leap into the world of **Yulimar Rojas Rodríguez**, the Venezuelan track and field athlete who has soared to incredible heights. Affectionately known as *"la Reina del Triple Salto"* (the Queen of the Triple Jump), Yulimar is a FOUR-TIME triple jump World Champion and THREE-TIME World Indoor Champion, as well as being the first Venezuelan woman ever to win an Olympic medal.

Growing up, Yulimar excelled in sports like track, volleyball, and basketball, but could not find nearby teams, so she pursued athletics. As a teenager, she dominated the high jump, shot put, sprinting, and the triple jump.

However, Yulimar's family struggled financially and she needed access to the best resources, including better food and medical treatment, to stay healthy and reach her full potential. In 2015, she moved to Spain to continue her training. Despite many setbacks along the way, this move gave Yulimar the chance she needed to push her career to the next level.

Yulimar won first place in the triple jump in the 2016 World Indoor Championships, the 2017 World Championship, the 2018 World Indoor Championships, and the 2019 World Championships. She won gold in the triple jump at the 2021 Tokyo Olympics, setting a new Olympic *and* **world record**. In 2022 and 2023, she maintained her first-place wins and secured her **third consecutive** Diamond League title.

Beyond her athletic achievements, Yulimar is an LGBTQ+ activist and a proud lesbian who speaks out for progress in Venezuela.

Her story is one of triumph, breaking barriers, and inspiring a nation. She said, *"This is only the beginning for Yulimar Rojas and Venezuela. Many more medals will come to this beautiful country... I love my country. Long live Venezuela!"*

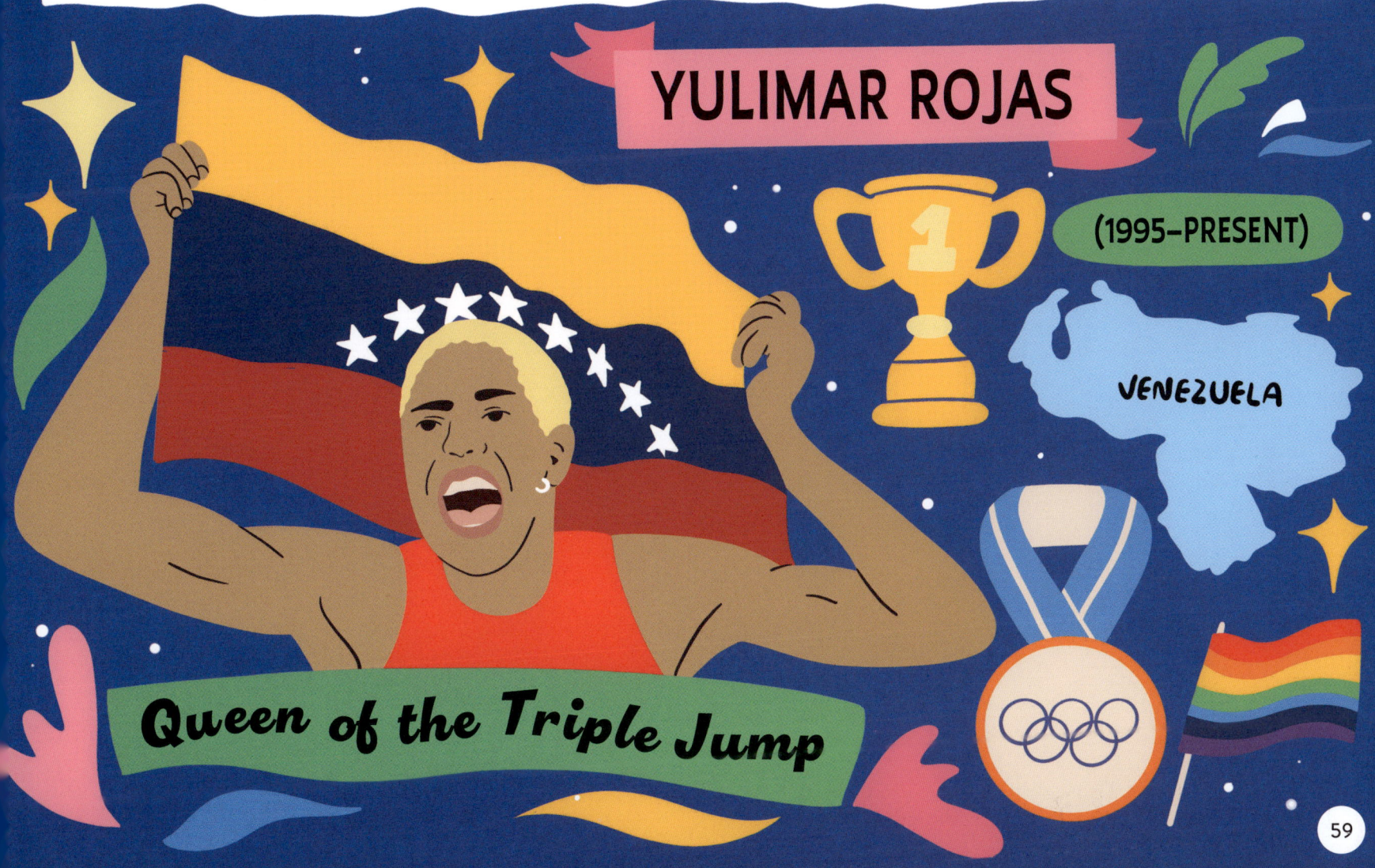

**YULIMAR ROJAS**

(1995–PRESENT)

VENEZUELA

**Queen of the Triple Jump**

# LAURIE HERNANDEZ

## (2000-PRESENT)

U.S.A.

PUERTO RICO

*Trailblazing Gymnast*

**Laurie Zoe Hernandez** is a Puerto Rican-American artistic gymnast who has tumbled, flipped, and soared her way to greatness. She is an Olympic athlete and has been celebrated in the New Jersey Hall of Fame.

Laurie's professional gymnastics journey began when she was 12 years old. She burst onto the scene with a silver medal in the all-around (the combined score for all four gymnastics apparatus: vault, bars, balance beam, and floor) at a competition called **the U.S. Classic**. Laurie's team won gold at the International Junior Mexican Cup, and she won the silver medal in the all-around.

But her path wasn't all smooth flips and perfect landings; Laurie faced challenges, including a fractured wrist and a torn tendon with a dislocated kneecap. She bounced back with determination. At the 2016 Rio Olympics, she helped the U.S. team win the gold medal while winning gold herself on the beam, silver on the vault, and bronze in the all-around.

Her amazing talents extend beyond gymnastics. Laurie is an exceptional dancer and won the television show *Dancing with the Stars*. She has also authored two books, *I Got This: To Gold and Beyond* (which was a *New York Times* bestseller) and an inspirational children's book called *She's Got This*.

Laurie has been honest and vulnerable about her struggles with depression and the eating disorders that she developed after being abused by a former coach. She spoke out against the coach to protect future gymnasts and her bravery ensured that justice was served.

As a proud Puerto Rican athlete, Laurie knows she is an important role model and she always strives to inspire girls to follow their dreams.

Lights, camera, action on Puerto Rican-Mexican-American actor **Jenna Marie Ortega**!

Growing up with five siblings in California, Jenna dreamed of becoming an actor from the age of six. Her parents supported her dreams, and her mother, who worked long hours as an emergency room nurse, would drive Jenna on the six-hour journey to Los Angeles for auditions up to **FIVE** days a week.

Jenna faced tremendous rejection, often because there were too few roles for Latinas. She didn't have any connections in the film and TV industry, and only landed parts in commercials. However, she turned her challenges into motivation and determination, and she finally landed her breakthrough role as young Jane in the comedy-drama *Jane the Virgin*. She then won an Imagen Award for her leading role as Harley Diaz, a hopeful inventor in Disney's *Stuck in the Middle*.

Despite this success, Jenna almost quit acting because it was difficult to transition from younger to more mature roles. She persevered, and finally landed a successful role as a headstrong teen seeking more independence from her parents in the film *Yes Day*.

Jenna was recognized by the Golden Globe, Primetime Emmy, and Screen Actors Guild awards for her iconic portrayal of Wednesday Addams in the series *Wednesday*. She initially rejected the role because she wanted to focus on films, but reconsidered. Jenna immersing herself in the role by reading the original comics, watching the TV adaptation, and learning to speak German.

Jenna Marie Ortega's journey from a determined six-year-old dreamer to a Hollywood sensation is an inspiration to would-be actors everywhere!

**3**

JENNA ORTEGA

(2002–PRESENT)

MEXICO

PUERTO RICO

U.S.A.

*Film and TV Superstar*

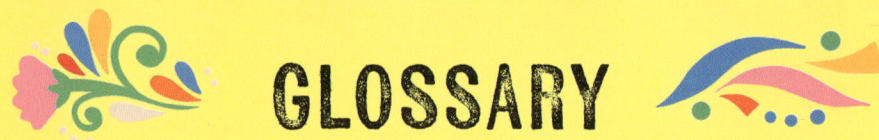

# GLOSSARY

**Activist**   Someone who takes action to make the world a better place. An activist is like a superhero for good causes, like caring for the planet and treating everyone fairly.

**All-around (gymnast)**   Gymnasts compete on the vault, bars, balance beam, and floor. The gymnast with the highest combined score wins.

**Baseliner (in tennis)**   A player who usually stays near the back line of the court, called the "baseline," instead of running up close to the net.

**Biochemistry**   The study of tiny building blocks called molecules, which make up everything. Biochemists figure out how these tiny molecules interact and team up to create life.

**Black Hole**   A hole in space that forms when a giant star dies and its gravity gets so strong that it pulls everything nearby into it, like a super-strong vacuum. Even light can't escape it.

**Capitalism**   An economic system in which private individuals and/or corporations determine the production, distribution, and exchange of goods and services in order to create wealth.

**Climate Change**   The Earth getting warmer over time, causing unusual weather, like stronger storms, droughts, or melting ice in the polar regions.

**Computer Scientists**   Experts who write special codes and programs to tell computers to do incredible things, like creating games, apps, and websites. They also solve puzzles to make computers smarter.

**Congress**   A group of politicians that make important decisions for the U.S.A. They represent different states and are elected by the people who live there. There are two groups: **the Senate** and **the House of Representatives**.

**Couturier**   A fashion designer who manufactures and sells clothes that have been tailored to a customer's specific requirements and measurements. This clothing is **couture**.

**Dark matter**   A mysterious substance that scientists believe is all around us in space, but we can't see it with telescopes because it doesn't give off any light. Even though we can't see it directly, we know it's there because we can see its effects on things like stars and galaxies.

**Depression**   A sad feeling that can make it hard for someone to enjoy things they used to love, feel interested in life, or have the energy to do daily things. People can get help by talking to a counselor or seeing a doctor.

**Diamond League**   A big sports league for some of the world's best track and field athletes. They compete in events all over the world, like running races, jumping, and throwing. The winners earn diamond-shaped trophies.

**Dictator**   Someone who has all the power in a country and makes all the important decisions. They can tell people what they're allowed to say and do. Most people are scared to challenge or oppose them.

**Diplomat**   A person appointed by a government to maintain political, economic, and social relations with other countries.

**Diverse**   Having lots of different kinds of people, ideas, or things. For example, a diverse group of friends might include people with different backgrounds or cultures. Or, a diverse garden has many types of flowers, plants, and colors.

**Eating Disorder**   A serious health problem where someone has a tough relationship with food and eating. Doctors, counselors, and loved ones can all help those with eating disorders.

**Economic**   The way people and businesses use money and resources.

**Entrepreneur**   Someone who runs a business or multiple businesses.

**Equality**   When everyone is treated fairly and given the same chances, no matter who they are.

**FEMA (the Federal Emergency Management Agency)** A group who make sure that if a disaster happens, like a hurricane, there's a plan to keep everyone safe and well.

**Gravitational Waves**   Ripples in space from something really heavy, like a planet or two black holes. Scientists have special space detectors that can feel and measure

gravitational waves to learn more about the universe and how things in space move and interact, even if they're far away.

**Hadron Collider**   A giant machine that helps scientists understand tiny particles like atoms.

**Honorary Doctorate**   A degree given by a college or university to someone who is not a student but who has done something important.

**Humanitarian**   Someone working to help others by promoting human welfare and social reform.

**LGBTQ+**   A term that describes different groups of people based on who they love and how they feel about their gender. The letters stand for:
**Lesbian:** Women who love women
**Gay:** Men who love men
**Bisexual:** People who love both men and women
**Transgender:** People whose gender identity is different from what they were assigned at birth
**Queer or Questioning:** People who don't fit into the usual categories or are figuring out their identity
**+** includes the other identities and experiences that aren't included in those letters, like non-binary.
It's important to treat everyone with kindness and respect, no matter their identity.

**Non-binary**   People who don't feel like they fit into just being a boy or a girl.

**Patent**   A legal right that enables the owner of intellectual property to exclude others from making, using, or selling an invention for a limited period of time.

**Philanthropist**   Someone who cares about helping other people and making the world a better place. They use their time, money, and/or resources to do good things for others.

**Philologist**   Someone who studies the history of languages.

**Philosopher**   People who use their brains to think about really big and challenging questions, like "What is the meaning of life?"

**Protest**   A group of people coming together in a public place, like a park or the street, to speak up about something they believe in. Protests are a way for people to peacefully show that they want things to be different or better.

**Producer**   Someone who helps make movies, TV shows, or music. They are in charge of making sure everything goes smoothly, like finding the right actors, managing the money, and planning the schedule for filming or recording.

**Ready-to-wear**   Clothes that are made in a factory and sold for people to buy and wear right away, without needing any special fitting or changes. This is the opposite of couture.

**Simulate**   To make something look like something else.

**STEM**   Science, Technology, Engineering, and Math.

**Telenovelas**   Popular TV shows that tell a story full of drama, romance, and sometimes comedy. Telenovelas often come from countries in Latin America and are usually in Spanish, but they can be enjoyed by anyone.

The terms "Hispanic" and "Latine" are related to ethnicity and identity, and their meanings can vary based on individual perspectives and preferences. Here's a general understanding:

**Hispanic:** Typically refers to people with a cultural or historical connection to Spain or Spanish-speaking countries. It is widely used in the U.S.A. to categorize people. The issue with this term is that some people find that "Hispanic" emphasizes a connection to the Spanish language and Spain instead of the diverse cultures in Latin America and the Caribbean.
**Latine:** A more inclusive term used to identify those of Latin American and/or Caribbean descent. It attempts to address some of the limitations associated with "Hispanic." Unlike the terms Latino/Latina, it is also gender-neutral and emphasizes a shared identity based on Latin American and Caribbean roots rather than language or colonial history.

Importantly, preferences for identity terms are personal. People's choices in identifying with these terms can vary, and it's crucial to use the terms that individuals themselves prefer. Understanding and respecting the diversity within the Latin American and Caribbean communities is vital in using these terms appropriately.

To all Latine and Hispanic readers, I hope you draw inspiration from these heroes. Discover your gifts and dreams. Be bold and brilliant. — A. R-M.

To my friends Magu, Jofi, Lucía, and everyone from Las Pochas for endlessly embracing me, supporting me, and always pushing me forward. — S. C.

First Published in 2025 by Wide Eyed Editions,
an imprint of The Quarto Group.
100 Cummings Center, Suite 265D, Beverly, MA 01915, USA.
T +1 978-282-9590 www.Quarto.com
EEA Representation, WTS Tax d.o.o., Žanova ulica 3, 4000 Kranj, Slovenia.

ISBN 978-0-7112-9436-3

The illustrations were created digitally.
Set in Semplicita Pro, Caffeine and Chill Script

Designer: Lyli Feng
Commissioning Editor: Hannah Dove
Editors: Hannah Dove and Katie Taylor
Production Controller: Dawn Cameron
Art Director: Karissa Santos
Publisher: Debbie Foy

Manufactured in Guangdong, China TT032025

9 8 7 6 5 4 3 2 1